WOMAN IN ISLAM

WOMAN IN ISLAM

Murtaḍā Muṭahharī

Translated by
M. A. Ansari

Copyright © 2021 by MIU PRESS

All rights reserved. No part of this publication may be reproduced, distributed, or transmitted in any form or by any means, including photocopying, recording, or other electronic or mechanical methods, without the prior written permission of the publisher, except in the case of brief quotations embodied in critical reviews and certain other noncommercial uses permitted by copyright law. For permission requests, write to the publisher, Shia Books Australia addressed "Attention: - Permissions (Women in Islam)," at the email address below.

All moral obligations of the authors have been met

A catalogue record for this book is available from the British Library and the Australian National Library

Ordering Information:
Quantity sales. Special discounts are available on quantity purchases by corporations, associations, and others. For details, contact the distributor at the address below.

Shia Books Australia
www.shiabooks.com.au
info@shiabooks.com.au

ISBN 978-1-911361-03-9

This English edition first published in 2016
Second Edition 2021

Contents

Transliteration VII
Preface IX
Prologue 1
Preface of the Author 9
Islam and Modern Life 13
The Flexibility of Islamic Laws 23
Woman's Rights in Islam and in the West 29
The Human Position of Woman according to the
Holy Qur'an 37
Natural Postulates of Family Rights 41
Disparities between Man and Woman 44
Study of Islamic Rules Concerning Woman 49
Proposal 50
Fixed-Time Marriage 51
Benefits of Fixed-Time Marriage 54
Social Causes of ' ' Formation 59
Has Fixed-Time Marriage Been Made Lawful to
Satisfy Lust? 60
Woman and Social Independence 63
Dower and Maintenance 67
Inheritance 83
Divorce 86
Some Theories about Divorce 87

CONTENTS

Polygamy 101
Sexual Communism 101
Polyandry 102
Polygamy 103
Historical Causes of Polygamy 104
Drawbacks and Defects of Polygamy 117
From the Psychological Angle 117
From the Angle of Behavior 118
From the Moral Angle 119
From the Legal Angle 120
From the Philosophical Angle 121
.... 122
Index 127

Transliteration

Symbol	Transliteration	Symbol	Transliteration
ء	ʾ	أ	a
ب	b	ت	t
ث	th	ج	j
ح	ḥ	خ	kh
د	d	ذ	dh
ر	r	ز	z
س	s	ش	sh
ص	ṣ	ض	ḍ
ط	ṭ	ظ	ẓ
ع	ʿ	غ	gh
ف	f	ق	q
ك	k	ل	l
م	m	ن	n
ه	h	و	w
ي	y	ة	ah

Long Vowels		Short Vowels	
آ	ā	َ	a
اى	ī	ِ	i
او	ū	ُ	u

Persian Letters			
Symbol	Transliteration	Symbol	Transliteration
پ	p	چ	ch
ژ	zh	گ	g

At the end of Farsi words, 'eh', '-e', and '-ye' have been used.

Preface

Among the issues occupying Master Muṭahharī's mind and thoughts for a long time were the dubieties concerning the matter of woman and her rights in Islam. In the introduction to his book *'Adl Ilāhī* (Divine Justice), written in 1352 S.A.H., he writes, "In the last three to four years, I have dedicated a considerable portion of my time to Islamic problems concerning women and their rights; several such works of mine have been published as a series of articles in journals or as books. The reason why I spent time on this matter was that I felt that the problem is not just the deviations that have practically emerged in this matter; the main issue is that in their speeches, class lectures, books, and essays, some present an incorrect image of the opinions of Islam concerning the rights of women and the boundaries of their duties, turning them into instruments of propaganda against Islam, and unfortunately the masses in the Islamic society are not at all familiar with Islam's logic in such matters as well as others. Thus, unfortunately a large number of people, including both men and women, have been made pessimistic toward Islam. Therefore, I found it necessary to clarify Islam's logic regarding this matter, so that it would become clear that not only is the logic of Islam flawless, but the well-founded and robust logic of Islam with regard to women, their rights, and the boundaries of their duties serves as the greatest proof of Islam's authenticity and legitimacy as well as its superhuman aspect."

It was on this basis that he endeavored to author certain works on this matter, the most significant of which being the books *Niẓām-e Ḥuqūq-e Zan dar Islam* (the system of woman rights in Islam), *Mas'ali-ye Ḥijāb* (the issue of *Ḥijāb*), and *Akhlāq-e Jinsī dar Islam* (gender-related ethics in Islam).

The background of the compilation of the book *Niẓām-e Ḥuqūq-e Zan dar Islam*, is as follows: as the master points out, 1345 S.A.H. witnessed the emergence in periodicals, especially women magazines, of a craze for changing the civil laws concerning family rights. Amidst the heat, a man named Ibrāhīm Mahdawī Zanjānī, who manifested the greatest zeal in this matter, composed a bill consisting of forty articles and published it in the *Zan-e Rūz* magazine, promising to present a well-reasoned defense of his opinions through a series of essays. Since many of his suggestions were in a clear opposition to definite statements of the Quran, an official, who was a clergyman, contacted Master Muṭahharī and informed him of this matter; following a series of arguments, it was decided that the magazine in question publish the essays written by Master Muṭahharī in criticism of the said person's opinions and defense of Islamic views along with the essays written by the person in question. The first essay was published in the 88th volume of the said magazine in Ābān 1345 S.A.H.; after six weeks, however, Mr. Mahdawī Zanjānī died of a heart attack. After that, since his essays had met with a considerable reception, Master Muṭahharī was asked to continue his essays individually, the result of which were 33 essays published in the magazine.

From the 6th essay onward, through a number of essays Master Muṭahharī deals with the theory and basics of Islam concerning the matter in question, and once they are completed he proceeds to deal with the rest of the problems posed regarding other aspects. In order to observe the logical order of the discussion, here a summary of the said theoretical discussions comes first. Briefly and in a single division, one may divide master's discussions in the book into two parts: 1) theory and basics, and 2) answering criticisms and problems.

What Master Muṭahharī states in the first part is as follows:

A. The relation between Islam and modernization of life, and that Islamic laws possess a kind of flexibility which enables it to satisfy all individual and social needs of mankind in all ages through its constant and variable laws.

B. The position of women as humans in the Quran and Islam's opposition to degrading them.

C. The natural essentials of family rights, and that in order to recognize the rights of men and women one must pay attention to their differences and separate talents which are the result of their nature and their creation.

D. Discussing the differences between men and women with respect to their physique, mentality, and their emotions toward each other.

Taking the discussions of the first part as the basis, Master Muṭahharī deals with the criticisms made about woman rights in Islam. The basic problem regarding the rights of woman in Islam is that some think that "Islam is a man-centered religion which does not consider woman as a full-fledged human being and constantly views her with contempt; that in various cases it formulates its laws in a way that gives an advantage to men and oppresses women".

Master Muṭahharī managed to examine the above-mentioned criticisms and other minor ones concerning certain laws of Islam with regard to women, including the matters of marriage proposal, temporary marriage (*mut'a*), woman's social independence, dowry and allowance, inheritance, right to divorce, and polygamy. Later, in 1353 S.A.H., Master Muṭahharī published the 33 essays mentioned, along with a preface titled "*Niẓām-e Ḥuqūq-e Zan dar Islam*" (The system of woman rights in Islam), a work republished 28 times so far. In the preface to the very first publication, the master promised to publish in the second volume the criticisms related to the remaining problems as well as other notes, God-willing. The notes mentioned include the following subjects: the man's right to ruling the family; the right to have a child's custody; the waiting period after divorce *'idda* and its philosophy; woman and *ijtihād* and verdict giving; woman and politics; woman in judicial rules; woman in penal laws; woman's ethics and education; woman's covering and clothing; woman's gender-related ethics; the mother's position; woman and working outside the house; and certain other problems. Unfortunately, however, the master did not manage to carry out this task, and we hope that Ṣadrā Publications would publish the above-mentioned series as soon as possible, even if it is just in the form of the existent manuscripts.

The English translation of the book in question – i.e. *Woman and Her Rights in Islam* – translated by M. A. Ansari has been published before by Al-Mustafa International Research Institute (M.I.R.I) as well as some others. What is presented here to the audience, however, is an abridgement of the said work, aiming to make it comprehensible to a wider range of people who are interested in learning about or increasing their understanding of Islam and the rights of woman in Islam. This abridgement has been undertaken by the Office of Islamic Science Studies and Research in Imam Ṣādiq (A.S.) University.

Al-Mustafa International Research Institute (M.I.R.I) is

PREFACE

honored to present this book to the valuable readers in a new form, it has been, however, briefly edited, its words have been transliterated and various indexes and bibliography have been added to it.

We hope that this book will be a valuable contribution to Islamic thought that is of value to the general reader and the researcher alike.

We take this opportunity to express our gratitude to "Islam and West Research Centre Ltd" for publishing this book and hope that the latter should form a link showing the way for those who seek advancement.

Al-Mustafa International Research Institute (M.I.R.I.)

Prologue

According to our view, the most fundamental question, or at least one of the most fundamental questions, in respect of family rights, is whether the domestic system is independent of all other social systems and has its own special criteria and logic, or it is just one out of many social systems and the same criteria and philosophy apply to it as are applied to all other social systems, or there is no difference between this social unit and others.

The basis of the doubt is that, on the one hand, in this system the main parties concerned belong to two opposite sexes, and on the other, it involves the propagation and procreation of the progeny. Nature has made the physical characteristics as well as the reproductive organs of the two parties dissimilar. Domestic society is semi-natural and semi-contractual.

There is evidently a doubt that whether natural and human rights of woman and man are similar or not.

In the Western world, a movement for human rights

emerged in the 17th century, in the wake of scientific and philosophical movements. The writers and thinkers of the 17th and the 18th centuries such as Jean Jacques Rousseau, Voltaire and Montesquieu made commendable efforts in giving currency to their ideas regarding the natural, undeniable and inalienable human rights.

Their basic idea was that human beings have a series of natural and inborn rights and freedoms which are absolutely inalienable and untransferable and cannot be renounced by anyone under any pretext and all people enjoy these rights equally.

The result of this social and intellectual movement first manifested itself in England, then in America and afterwards in France and together with new developments led to the appearance of socialism in the 19th Century.

Till the end of the 19th century, all talks and whatever practical steps were taken in human rights sphere, were mostly confined to the rights of the nations as regards the governments and the employees versus the employers. In the 20th century, the question of women's rights was raised and for the first time in 1948, the United Nations' Universal Declaration of Human Rights proclaimed the equality of rights between man and woman in clear terms.

All social movements in the West since the 17th century had revolved around liberty and equality. As the movement for women's rights was the latest in the series, and the history of women's lot in Europe, from this point of view, was extraordinarily bitter, the UN's Declaration of Human Rights talked of nothing but liberty and equality.

The protagonists of this movement maintained that it was complementary to the movement for human rights. They held that without ensuring women's liberty and equality it was meaningless to talk of human liberty and human rights. They further asserted that the main cause of all domestic troubles was that woman was deprived of her liberty and equality with man, and that all domestic problems would be solved once this aspect was taken care of.

What, in this connection, was overlooked was what we have described as 'the fundamental question regarding the system of family rights', that is, whether this system is, or is not, independent of other social systems, and whether it has or has not, different criteria and logic. Attention was concentrated only on the general principles of liberty and equality, and the only point taken into consideration was that of natural and inalienable human rights. It was argued that woman, as a human being, was entitled to all the rights enjoyed by man.

Perhaps apathy on this vital question is due to the hasty development of the women's liberation movement. That is why, while this movement has redressed certain grievances of women, in certain other respects it has caused calamity to them as well as to the human society as a whole. In this movement, it was forgotten that equality and liberty were two necessary but not sufficient conditions to fulfil woman's rights. Woman, as a human being, is born free like any other human being and in that capacity she has equal rights. But woman is a human being with certain peculiarities, as man is a human being with certain other peculiarities. The traits of their characters are different and their mentality is distinct. This difference is not the result of any geographical, historical or social factors, but lies in the very making of them. Nature has purposely made them different and any action taken against the intention of nature would produce a disastrous result. We should seek guidance from nature itself to decide whether the rights of man and woman are of the same kind rights. During this movement, intentionally or unintentionally, equality has been used in the sense of similarity and thus quality has overshadowed quantity. It was stressed that a woman is a human being, but it was forgotten that she is a woman too.

In fact, this indifference was not the outcome of mere haste; there were other factors also, which impelled the exploitation of woman in the name of liberty.

One of them was the excessive greed of the industrialists, who wanted to lure woman from her house to a factory, in order to exploit her economic potentiality. For this purpose, they advocated woman's rights, her economic independence and her liberty and equality of rights with those of man. As Will Durant says 'female workers were cheaper and the employers preferred them to strong-headed and costly male workers. A century ago, it was hardly possible for men to get a job, but there were advertisements asking them to send their women-folk and children to the factories. The first step towards the emancipation of women was taken in 1882, when a law was enacted according to which the women of Great Britain acquired an unprecedented privilege of keeping with themselves whatever money they earned.[1] This law, described to be in keeping with high moral values of Christianity, was passed by the mill-owners and the House of Commons, to lure the women of England to the factories.[2]

With the development of machines and the ever-increasing growth of production it became necessary for the capitalists that, in order to impose their surplus products on the consumers, and to convert the consumers into consumption factors and to make them as powerless tools in consumption market once again the

---

1. Dr. ʿAlī Shāygān, in his commentary on the Iranian Civil Code, writes that the independence, in respect of property, which a woman enjoys now and which has been recognized by the *Shīʿah* law from the very beginning, did not exist in ancient Greece, Rome, Germany and till recently in most of the other countries. She, like a minor and a lunatic, was interdicted from the disposition of her property. In England, where previously her personality was completely merged with that of her husband, two laws were enacted, one in 1870 and the other in 1882, which removed inhibitions regarding the ownership of property by a married woman. (ʿAlī Shāygān, *Ḥuqūq Madanī Iran*, Tehran: Majlis, 1324 S.A.H.).

2. William James Durant, *The Pleasures of Philosophy,(Ladhdhāt Falsafeh)*, trans. ʿAbbās Zaryāb Khūʾī, (Tehran: Andīsheh, 1344 S.A.H).

services of women to be utilized, but not as simple workers. They, on the other hand, exploited their beauty, charm and sexual attraction in the name of freedom for women.

Politics also did not lag behind in utilizing this factor. You regularly read such reports in the newspapers and magazines. Woman is exploited and her services are used to fulfill the objects of men under the cloak of liberty and equality. The youth of the 20th century could not miss this valuable opportunity. In order to allure her, without shouldering conventional responsibilities, and to prey upon her freely, he, more than anyone else, shed crocodile tears for women's helplessness and the undue discrimination against her. To be able to make a greater contribution to this 'sacred cause,' he went to the extent of delaying his own marriage till the age of 40 or even remaining single forever.

The present century has rectified many grievances of woman, but it has also brought many misfortunes to her. Are women condemned to one of these two sufferings and must be compelled to choose one of these two ways or is there a third way? In fact, it is not at all necessary that she should continue to suffer. She suffered in the past, mostly because it was forgotten that she was a human being. She is suffering now because her womanhood, her inborn requirements, her natural rights and demands and her special capabilities have been ignored, intentionally or otherwise. It should be noted that natural differences between woman and man does not show woman's imperfection or that nature has been unkind towards her. If we adopt a position based on such differences, we will not be unjust; rather, in fact, it is the disregard of woman's natural position which mostly leads to her being deprived of her rights. If men form a front against women they say: 'As both of us are equal, our work, responsibilities, rewards and retributions must be similar. You must share with us in our hard and heavy jobs, take wages according to the amount of the work you perform and must not expect any consideration, respect or protection...'

If such a situation arises, women may be the losers, because by nature they have a less productive capacity, while their consumption of wealth is more than men's. Their menstrual cycles, hardships of pregnancies, pains of childbirth and the nursing of children place them in a position in which they require men's protection. They are in need of more rights and cannot afford to have less commitments. This position is not peculiar to human beings. It applies to all animals living in pairs. In the case of all such animals the male instinctively protects its female partner. Thus, to recognize rights of woman and man, we have to take into account natural position of each of them. Nowadays, women in the western society are protesting against this situation, since they are so fed up with the discomforts which have been imposed upon them in the name of liberty and equality that they have become allergic to these two words. They forget that the words are not to be blamed. Man and woman are two stars with their distinct orbits within which they should move.

> It is not given to the sun to overtake the moon, nor can the night outpace the day. Each in its orbit floats. (36:40)

Liberty and equality can be useful only if both the sexes follow their normal and natural courses.

We believe that the question of women's rights at home and in the society should be re-evaluated. We should be guided by nature and should take into consideration all the bitter and sweet experiences of the past, especially of the present century. Only then will the movement for women's rights be reasonable in the real sense.

It is admitted by every friend and foe that the Holy Qur'an revived the rights of women. The Qur'an revived the rights of woman as a human being and man's partner in humanity and human rights, but did not overlook her womanhood or man's manhood. In other words, the Qur'an did not overlook woman's nature. That is why complete harmony exists between the dictates of nature and the dictates of the Qur'an. The woman in the Qur'an is the same as the woman in nature. These two great divine books, one created and the other compiled, fully conform to each other. The main aim of our book is to highlight and explain this harmony.

Preface of the Author

In the name of Allah, the Beneficent, the Merciful

In this writing, I seek to discuss a part of the social philosophy of Islam. As I have said many times, I do not like to defend the Civil Code and say that it is complete and in full correspondence to the Islamic laws and correct social standards; nor do I want to claim that the method popular among majority of our people is right and in correspondence to justice. On the contrary, I find disorders in family relations and believe that some fundamental improvements should be made. In this way, unlike some groups, I do not seek to fully acquit Iranian men and I do not consider the Civil Code as the main guilty. Nor do I consider the Civil Code as following the Islamic jurisprudence. Rather, I prove that, in this field, Islamic laws are in harmony with accurate psychological, natural, and social considerations; and dignity and nobility of woman and man have been equally taken into account in them; and if these laws are implemented, they will be the best guarantee for the health of family.

PREFACE OF THE AUTHOR

Now, and before beginning to discuss the above issues, some points should be noted:

The problem of family relations in our times is not so simple that it may be resolved by arranging opinion polls of young boys and girls, or by holding seminars. It is neither confined to any one country, nor has any country so far claimed to have solved it successfully.

Even now, we, more than ever, hear complaints that the domestic system is collapsing, the basis of matrimony is weakening, the young men are evading marriage, the young women are hating motherhood, the relations between the parents (especially mothers) and the children are deteriorating, modern woman is getting vulgar, love is being replaced with cheap sensuality, cases of divorce are ever growing, the number of children born of unregistered wedlock or marital ties not formally legalized is on the increase and sincerity, respect and cordiality between husband and wife are becoming rare.

It is regrettable that some of the misinformed people think that the questions related to family relations are similar to the industrial problems to solve them we should follow the Westerners. Some people think that the deterioration and corruption of the family system is due to women's liberation which, in turn, is the unavoidable result of industrial life and the progress of science and civilization. It is a question of compulsion of history. We have no alternative but to submit to this corruption and chaos, and to forget all about the domestic happiness which we enjoyed before.

This way of thinking is very superficial and childish. We admit that industrial life has affected family relations and is still affecting it, but the main factors, which have disrupted family life in Europe, are two: 'One of them consists of the foolish and cruel customs, usages and laws which were prevalent in Europe till a century ago. It was only at the end of the 19th century and the beginning of the 20th century that women in Europe secured the right of ownership of property. The other factor is that those who undertook to improve the position of women chose a wrong path: They intended to beautify her eyebrows, but deprived her of her eyesight!' More than the industrial life, the old laws of Europe and the reforms of the modernists are responsible for the present chaos and confusion. We should look at the western life cautiously. While utilizing and acquiring their sciences, industries, techniques and some commendable and imitable social regulations we should refrain from imitating.

1. What that has been proposed to make changes in the Civil Code while it is against Islamic laws and in conflict with psychological and social requirements, do not correspond to the Constitution; for it has been said that no 'law' can be enacted which is in conflict with Islamic laws. Apart from religion, the Constitution itself is sacred for people of the country.

2. Even if we put aside such proposals which are in conflict with the Constitution, it cannot be denied that, in the present time, the strongest emotion ruling mentalities of Iranians is the religious one. How may such 'laws' be brought in harmony with such a psychological and emotional background? Religious conscience of people cannot be changed through making changes in laws or enacting new laws. Such laws either become useless as a result of the influence of religion and prevalence of conscience or, after some psychological skirmishes, weaken religious power.

3. Nevertheless suspicions posed against Islam make me, unlike many people, happy in spite of my interest and belief in Islam. For I believe that this holy religion has emerged stronger than before in every front in which it has been attacked. It is the characteristic of truth that doubt and suspicion help to clarify it. Doubt is the first step towards certainty. Let's they say, write, hold seminars, and pose objections and unwillingly become a means by which Islamic truths may be clarified.

Islam and Modern Life

The question of religion and modernity is one of those subjects which do not concern the Muslims alone. Other religions also had to face this question. Many liberal minded people in the world have renounced religion, because they are under the impression that religion and modern life are incompatible. They think that inertia, stagnation and rigidity are the inherent properties of religiousness. For example, we may mention the late Mr. Nehru, the former Prime Minister of India, who had been averse to religion because of its rigidity and monotony. Towards the end of his life Nehru felt a vacuum within himself and in the world and believed that it could be filled only by a spiritual force. But still, he was not inclined to accept any religion, because he believed that a state of rigidity and monotony pervaded all religions.

Of all the religions Islam alone is more concerned with all the aspects of human life. Its teachings are not confined to acts of worship and prayer and to a set of moral counsels. As Islam has dealt with men's relations with God, it has also given the broad lines of men's relations with each other, so that many non-Muslim intellectuals and writers have studied the social and civil laws of Islam and have commended them as a body of progressive laws and recognized the applicability of its laws to all times and circumstances. For example, Bernard Shaw has said:

> It [Islam] is the only religion which appears to me to possess that assimilating capability to the changing phase of existence, which can make itself appeal to every age. I believe that if a man like him [Muḥammad] were to assume the leadership of the modern world, he would succeed in solving its problems in a way that would bring it the much needed peace and happiness.[1]

During our time the question, whether Islam is compatible with the present age, has become a burning question.

Sometimes they give a philosophical turn to their query and say that everything in this world is subject to change. Nothing is static and stationary, human society being no exception. Then, how can a body of laws remain unchanged through the ages? If we look at this question from a purely philosophical point of view, the answer is simple. It is the material things of the world which are ever changing; which grow and decline, and which are

---

1. George Bernard Shaw in: *'The Genuine Islam,'* Vol. 1, No. 8, 1936.

subject to evolution and decay. As for the universal laws, they do not change. For example, all living things have evolved and continue to evolve according to certain laws which have been set forth by the scientists. The living things themselves are, no doubt, ever changing, but the laws of their evolution and development are not subject to any change. Anyhow, the queries in respect of the compatibility and incompatibility of Islam with the requirements of the time do not have a general and philosophical aspect alone.

The question, which is more often asked, is that when the laws are framed to meet human requirements which are not constant, how can social laws be constant and unalterable?

Incidentally, it is a miraculous characteristic of Islam that it provides constant laws to meet all constant requirements of the individuals and the society, and flexible laws for the temporary and changing requirements.

Before going into this question we should like to bring forward two points:

The first point is that most of the people who talk of progress, development and change in a situation suppose that any social change, especially if its source is in the West, is the consequence of progress and development. These people are under the impression that as the means of life change from day to day, and the imperfect ones are replaced by the perfect ones and as science and industry are constantly advancing, all changes in human life are a sort of progress and advancement and should be welcomed as such. Not only that, they think that such changes are inevitable and have to come with the passage of time.

In fact, all changes are not the direct result of the advancement of science and industry, nor are they inevitable. While science is progressing, the selfish and animal nature of man is also not idle and pushes him towards corruption and perversion. We have to march forward with the advancement of time, but at the same time we must fight corruption also. If man should follow time and its changes with folded hands, then what will happen to the constructive and creative role of the human will? Man is riding the vehicle of time, which is in motion. He must not be negligent of guiding and controlling his vehicle. Otherwise, he will be like a person mounted on horseback, who leaves himself to the will of the horse.

The second point worth mentioning here is that some people have solved the difficult problem of 'Islam and the requirements of time' in a very simple and easy way. They say that Islam is an everlasting religion, and it can be adjusted to every age and every time. But when asked how this adjustment takes place and what its formula is, they at once say that when the circumstances change, the existing laws are repealed and replaced by other laws. Such people should be asked: If adjustability means capability of being repealed, which law does not have this type of flexibility? Is there any law which is not compatible with time in this sense? They say that the teachings of Islam are divided into three parts. The first part consists of basic doctrines, such as Divine Unity, Prophethood, Resurrection and etc. The second part is related to the acts of worship such as prayer, fasting, ablution, ritual cleaning, pilgrimage etc. The third part consists of the laws concerning the life of the people; and only the first two parts are an integral part of religion, and something to be preserved for ever. As far as the third part is concerned, it is not an integral part of religion. The Holy Prophet(S), as the Head of the State, had to give some laws also. Otherwise, religion has nothing to do with the worldly life of the people.

It is hard to believe that a person living in a Muslim country should be so ignorant of the precepts of Islam.

Has not the Qur'an described the aim of the Prophets and the Apostles?

The Qur'an describes social justice as the main aim of all the Prophets:

> We have sent Our Messengers with clear proof and We have sent down with them the Book and the Balance, so that people may rise with justice. (57:25)

Most of our misfortunes are due to the fact that our morals and laws have lost their only source of strength, viz. religion.

From the viewpoint of the West, the devotional rites of Islam must continue so that the Muslims, whenever need be, could be stirred up against the atheistic and godless system of communism, but the social rules of Islam which provide a philosophy of life to the Muslims must go, for these rules give the Muslims a sense of independence and separate identity, and prevent their being swallowed up by the greedy West. They should be told that Islam, 1,400 years ago, depreciated the principle of, 'We believe in certain things (some of the teachings of Islam) and reject the others,' and proclaimed that the rules of Islam are irreversible and, when powerful, withstands any other system, whether it is atheistic or not. Islam wants to dominate the society as a philosophy of life. The Islam which will be restricted to the places of worship, will vacate the field, not only for the Western ideas, but it will vacate it for the anti-Western ideas and doctrines as well.

We said that, to discuss Islam and requirements if time and modern life, we have to study lives of human beings; and if we reflect upon this point, it will become clear that the social life of human beings is not an instinctive one, rather it is always subject to change.

There lies the secret of man's being the prince of creation. Human being is the mature and worthy child of nature. He has reached a stage, where he does not require the direct guidance of nature. In other words, he can lead a free life and that is the reason why he is not immune to mistakes, selfishness, ignorance and injustice. Where the

Qur'an refers to this wonderful human capacity, it also immediately describes man as 'unjust' and 'ignorant.' These two human capacities - the capacity of evolution and the capacity of deviation, are inseparable. On the other hand, man, in his life, sometimes goes forward and sometimes backward. It is one of the characteristics of man that he sometimes overacts and sometimes underacts. If he adopts the middle course, he endeavors to differentiate between the changes of the right type and that of the wrong type. He also tries to arrest perversion, and not to associate himself with it.

But unfortunately, man does not always adopt this course. The first disease results in stagnation and abstention from progress, and the second in perversion and ruin. The rigid is averse to everything new and cannot reconcile himself with anything, except the old. On the other hand, the misinformed regards everything new to be modern and progressive and considers it to be the requirement of time. He keeps his eyes fixed on the Western world to be able to imitate every new fashion and every new custom. He calls this modernity and the compulsion of time. Both the rigid and the misinformed suppose that all old customs and usages are a part of religious rites, with the difference that the rigid wants to preserve them, whereas the misinformed may conclude that religion is tantamount to stagnation and inertia. The question of contradiction between religion and science has been introduced for the first time in the West. The idea of contradiction arose from two developments. Firstly, the Church had accepted some ancient, philosophical and scientific notions as religious beliefs, but the progress of science has proved their falsity. Secondly, science has changed the form and the conditions of life. The uninformed and the misinformed people are also under the impression that religion has prescribed a particular form of material life, and as science has decreed a change in this form. And thus, they thought, there was a contradiction between science and religion and religion should be abolished.

Islam is opposed to both rigidity and ignorance, and regards both of them as dangerous. The Qur'an lays the foundation of a society, which is always growing, developing and expanding. The intellectual sterility of the rigid and their clinging to the old customs having no connection with Islam, have provided a pretext to the misinformed to consider Islam to be really opposed to modernity. On the other hand, the following and patronizing of the latest fashions and modes of the West by the misinformed, their belief that the prosperity of the people of the East depends on their complete westernization, both physically and spiritually, their acceptance of the habits, manners and traditions of the West, and the blind adaptation of their own civil and social laws to those of the Western nations, have provided a pretext to the rigid to look at everything new with suspicion and to regard it as a threat to their religion, to their independence and to the social personality of their community. In the meantime, Islam has to pay the penalty for the mistake of both the parties.

It is surprising that these so called cultured, but really ignorant people, think that time is infallible. To them, good and bad has no sense other than that of new and old. Feudalism is bad only because it has become old and has gone out of fashion. Otherwise, it was quite good when it was first introduced into the world. Similarly, exploitation of women or that women had no share of inheritance is bad only because it is disliked by the modern world. Otherwise, it was quite good when it was first introduced into the world! It should be noted that the use of heroin, the atom bomb and the blue films cannot be justified on the ground that they are among the phenomena of the present century. If the latest types of bombers are used for throwing the most perfect bombs on the people of another country, and the most highly educated people are employed to perform this job, can all this modernity reduce the inherent barbarity of the act?

The main argument of those, who say that in the matter of family rights we should follow the Western system, is that times have changed, and the requirements of the 20th century demand that we should do so. The changes, brought about by time, are sometimes progressive and sometimes retrogressive. We should march forward along with the progressive changes, and should fight the retrogressive tendencies. To distinguish between these two kinds of changes and to determine their nature, we should find out the source of the new developments, and which way they are directed to. We should see what human tendencies have brought them into existence, and which classes of society are behind them. We should see whether they have been motivated by high human tendencies or by low animal propensities, and whether they have come into existence as a result of selfless investigations of scholars and intellectuals, or have been motivated by the base desires of self-seekers and the corrupt elements of society.

The Flexibility of Islamic Laws

The second point, to be made clear, about Islam and requirements of Islam is 'what is the secret of Islam being in harmony with the expansion of knowledge and civilization, and the applicability of its firm and stable laws to the varying circumstances of life?'. We mention here only a few of them.

Islam has not dealt only with the external form of life, which depends upon the degree of the development of human knowledge. Islamic teachings are concerned also with the spirit and the goals of life, and determine the best way to reach these goals. Science has neither changed the spirit and the goals of life; and the external forms of these means may be chosen freely. Islam, by keeping only goals within its domain and leaving the form and means to the domain of science and technology, has avoided any clash with culture and civilization. Not only that, but by encouraging the factors helping the expansion of civilization, namely, knowledge, labor, piety, will, courage and perseverance, it has undertaken the role of the main factor working for the cause of the expansion of civilization. Islam has set up traffic signposts all along the route of human progress. They, on the one hand, indicate the route and the destination, and, on the other, warn against pitfalls and dangerous spots. The external and material forms of these means have no sanctity in Islam.

Islam has envisaged stable laws for the stable human requirements and varying laws for the varying requirements. A part of the human requirements, both individual and collective, is of a permanent nature. They do not undergo any change with the change of time. Another part of the human requirement is of a varying nature and this demands varying laws. To elucidate this point, I give a few examples:

Islam has laid down a social principle which has been stated in the Qur'an thus: 'Provide force against them (the enemies) to the utmost possible extent.' (8:60) The Prophet directed that the Muslims should learn the arts of horsemanship and archery and teach them to their children. It is quite obvious that the basic order is 'to provide force' as ordered by the above verse. However the necessity of acquiring skill in horsemanship and archery is a temporary requirement, which varies with the change of time. With the changed circumstances, skill in firearms etc. has taken the place of skill in archery.

Another example: Imām 'Alī (A.S.) never dyed his hair, though it had become grey during the last years of his life. One day a man said to him: 'Didn't the Prophet order grey hair to be covered with dye?' 'Yes, he did,' 'Alī replied. 'Then why don't you dye your hair?' the man asked. 'Alī said, 'At the time the Prophet gave that instruction the number of the Muslims was small, and there were many aged people who used to take part in the battles. The Prophet ordered them to dye their hair to conceal their real age, for if the enemy could see that he was faced with only a bunch of old men, his morale might have been raised. With the spread of Islam to the whole world, that situation has changed. Now everybody is free to dye, or not to dye, his hair.' Islam attaches importance to the external appearance, as well as to the inner spirit. But it wants the husk only for the sake of the kernel. Recently in some Islamic countries, there has been a controversy about the change of script. This question can be considered from two angles. The first is whether Islam favors any particular alphabet and discriminates against others; which is not, of course, the case, since Islam is a universal religion. The second form of the question is how far the change of script will lead to the cultural merger of a Muslim nation with the other peoples. And, it is in this respect that this question is of importance. Islam has not prescribed any particular design of shoes, cap or dress. What that Islam says is: 'Mimicry is forbidden. To be merged with others is forbidden. To be charmed by others is forbidden'.

Another aspect of Islam which makes it compatible with the requirements of the time is the conformity of its teachings to reason. Islam has proclaimed that its laws are based on considerations of higher interest. At the same time, Islam itself has given out the degree of importance of these interests. This facilitates the work of the experts of the Islamic law in those fields where various interests appear to be in contrast with each other. Islam has allowed the experts of Islamic law to weigh the relative importance of the various interests, and keeping in view the guidance which Islam itself has provided, to determine the more important interests. In Islamic jurisprudence, this rule is called the question as 'important and more important.'

1. Another aspect of Islam which has given this religion the characteristic of mobility and applicability to varying circumstances, and has kept it as a living and everlasting religion, is that within it there exists a body of laws whose object is to control and modify other laws. They are called by the jurists, 'the governing rules.' The rules of 'No harm' and 'No loss,' are among examples of such cases and govern all jurisprudence.

2. In addition, there is a further series of checks and balances which has given this religion the characteristic of finality. Āyatullah Nā īnī and 'Allāmah Ṭabāṭabā ī have, in this respect, mostly relied on the powers delegated by Islam to the righteous Islamic Government. On the other hand, Islam has a special aspect called *Ijtihād*. *Ijtihād* means expertise in Islamic matters. Ibn Sīnā (Avicenna) in

his book, *Al-Shifā*, says that conditions of life change constantly. New problems frequently crop up, but the fundamentals of Islam are constant and unalterable. Hence, in these circumstances, there should be some people who, with their full knowledge of all the points of law and precepts, may be able to answer all the questions which may arise from time to time, and thus meet the needs of the people. They are neither rigid and opposed to the modern developments, nor uninformed.

Woman's Rights in Islam and in the West

The followers of the Western systems assert that Islam is the religion of the male sex. It does not recognize woman to be a full human being. That is why it has not accorded her equal rights. Had it recognized her as a full human being, it would not have allowed polygamy; it would not have given man the right of divorce; it would not have fixed the share in inheritance of a female as half of the share of a male; it would not have ordered the naming of a price for woman under the name of dower, and would not have made woman dependent on man for maintenance, instead of making her economically and socially independent.

Thus, Islam has maintained legal privileges and preferences for men and has not taken into account the principle of equality.

To reply them, we say: we confirm that, since human dignity is common to man and woman, they both must enjoy the same rights and there should be no legal preference. The first question which comes to mind is whether equality of rights does really mean their similarity also. In fact, they are two different beings. Equality means a condition of being equal in degree and value, whereas similarity means uniformity. It is possible that a father may distribute his wealth among his three children equally, but not uniformly. Suppose his wealth consists of several items such as a commercial store, some agricultural land and some property, which has been leased out. He, taking into consideration their respective tastes and aptitudes, gives the store to one, the agricultural land to another and the leased property to the third. He takes care that what he gives to each of them should suit their aptitude.

Thus equality is other than uniformity. Equality is a charming word, for it implies a sense of indiscrimination. A particular sanctity is attached to it. Nowadays, however, it is mistakenly used instead of similarity. No doubt, Islam has not in all cases accorded similar rights to man and woman. But it has not also preferred men to women, which we will explain. There lies the difference between the Islamic view and the Western system that man and woman, because of the sex difference, should not be similar in respect of many rights and obligations. In the West, however, an attempt is being made to make their rights and obligations uniform, and to ignore their natural and innate differences. Thus, 'equality of rights' is only a forged label which has been attached to this

Western gift by the followers of the West. What we claim is that non-similarity of rights between man and woman is more in keeping with justice. It meets the requirement of natural rights better, ensures domestic happiness better and pushes society forward on the path of progress better. In other words, equality between woman and man requires dissimilarity between their rights.

The Muslim scholars, by expounding the principle of equity, laid the foundation of the philosophy of rights. It was the Muslims who, for the first time, paid attention to the question of human rights and the principle of equity, and set them forth as original and self-existing principles unaffected by any contractual law. But it was so destined that they could not continue their work and ultimately, after eight centuries, it was further developed by European intellectuals and philosophers, who appropriated the credit for it. The Europeans brought social, political and economic philosophies into existence, and acquainted nations with the value of life and human rights.

Apart from historical reasons, there was a psychological and regional reason too, which prevented the Muslim-East from pursuing the question of inherent rights which had been posed by the East itself.. The East is enamored of morals and the West of rights. The man of the East, because of his eastern nature, is seeking for his humanity in morals. But the man of the West is enamored of rights and seeks for his humanity in his rights and the way he defends them.

Islam has had and still has the big distinction of simultaneously paying attention to both the morals and the rights. Nevertheless, the Muslim East, though in the beginning it adopted both morals and rights from Islam, gradually left rights and restricted its attention to morals. Anyhow, at present we are concerned with the question of rights which may also be a philosophical question and needs to be dealt with at length. It is more closely related to the real meaning of justice and the true nature of rights - justice and rights which existed even when there was still no law in the world, and whose meanings cannot be changed by enacting any law. It is ridiculous to say that some countries want to ratify such rights in their Parliaments. After all, it is not within the jurisdiction of the Parliament of any country to ratify or reject the text of the Declaration of Human Rights. In fact, the Declaration of Human Rights is a philosophy and not a law. As such, it should be ratified by the philosophers and not by the legislators. Otherwise, why should a bill enunciating Einstein's theory of relativity not be introduced in some Parliament and passed by that august body? Whenever any declaration of rights is issued by a group of philosophers, every nation should refer it to its own thinkers and philosophers, and if it is approved by them only then all members of that nation are bound to abide by its provisions as extra legal facts. Even if some other nations are compelled to follow the majority of other nations in the matter of logic and philosophy and do not feel that they are competent enough to do any philosophical thinking themselves we Muslims must not follow their example. Further, as this question is not subject to test and trial, it does not require any such equipment or laboratory etc. as may be available to the Europeans only.

The important points of the preamble of the Declaration of Human Rights are as follows:

(i) All human beings enjoy inherent dignity and inalienable rights.

(ii) Human dignity and human rights are universal and indivisible. They pervade all human beings irrespective of race, color and sex. All human beings are members of a family, and hence none is superior to anyone else.

(iii) Full recognition of human dignity and inalienable human rights is the foundation of freedom, justice and peace.

(iv) The highest aspiration, for the materialization of which all must strive, is the emergence of a world in which freedom of belief, security and material welfare may be ensured and freedom from suppression, fear and poverty may be guaranteed. (v) Belief in human dignity and respect for inalienable human rights must be inculcated gradually in the minds of all, through teaching and education.

As the Declaration of Human Rights has been framed on the basis of respect for humanity, liberty and equality with a view to reviving human rights, it should be respected by every conscientious person. The basis of this Declaration is the inherent human dignity. It is here that the contradiction between the basis of the Declaration of Human Rights and the Western evaluation of man becomes evident The Western philosophy has since long depreciated man. Man, from the Western point of view, has come down to the position of a machine. According to the current European theory, belief in 'man as the crown of the creation' was only an offshoot of the now obsolete Ptolemaic astronomy, according to which the earth was believed to be the centre of the Universe and all the stars were believed to be revolving round it. Now that theory has gone, and, with its disappearance, no room is left for man's selfishness. The European does not believe that soul has any independent existence. In this respect he does not consider himself to be in any way different from a plant or an animal. Life for all living beings, including man, means a constant struggle for existence. This is the basic principle of life. Man has always been striving to be victorious in this struggle, and to save his position he has invented such moral rules as justice, virtue, co-operation, sincerity etc. From the standpoint of certain powerful Western schools of thought, man is just a machine which is actuated only by the motives of economic gains. Religion, morality, philosophy, science, literature and the arts are all superstructures. Western views have lowered his position from every angle. Having done all this, the Western countries have proclaimed a high-sounding

Declaration about human dignity and position and inalienable and sacred rights and have called upon mankind to enforce it. Though there are realist and fair ones among western philosophers, the prevalent idea in the West is what that we have just described.

The Declaration of Human Rights should have been issued by those, who consider man to be higher than a robot, who think that his motives are not limited to animal instincts and who have faith in human conscience. Only those who believe that man has a goal and a destination can talk of human rights.

> O men! Surely you have to labor and labor toward your Lord, and then you shall meet Him. (84:6)

What befits the Western way of thinking is not the Declaration of Human Rights but only the practical behavior of those Western people who kill all human sentiments, play with human characteristics, give preference to money over man, worship machinery, regard wealth as almighty and exploit other human beings and unlimited power of capitalism .....

Today's most important social question, in the words of the Holy Qur'an, is: Has man forgotten himself? He has confined his attention to the material world and has totally ignored introspection. He finds no goal in the creation unless enjoying material things and thinks that creation has no purpose. He thinks that he has lost his soul. Because of this way of thinking, true human beings should be always searched for in the past and the great system of the contemporary civilization is able to create everything except [true] human beings.

That is the reason why the Declaration of Human Rights is being violated by the West. The philosophy which is followed by the people of the West in their practical life makes the failure of the Declaration inevitable.

It became, thus, clear that what is inconsistent with the claim made by the West concerning the basis of the Declaration, is the way in which the West thinks about human beings. On the other hand, 'equality of the rights of woman and man' is a false name for what some people want in the form of similarity of woman and man in all aspects of life. Here the question arises as to what is the reason that in certain cases dissimilar rights have been accorded to man and woman. Would it not have been better, had their rights been similar, as well as equal in all cases? To give full consideration to this point, we propose to discuss it under three headings:

(i) The Islamic view of the position of woman from the angle of her nature.

(ii) The effect of the physical disparity between man and woman. Does it make them dissimilar in the matter of rights also?

(iii) What is the philosophy behind the Islamic rules, which are in some cases different in respect of man and woman? Is this philosophy still valid?

The Human Position of Woman according to the Holy Qur'an

The Qur'an is not merely a collection of laws. It contains laws, as well as history, religious exhortations, an explanation of the meaning of Creation. ... The Qur'an is not a book of philosophy, but it has expounded, in very definite terms, its views on the three basic subjects of philosophy: the world, man and society. It does not teach its followers law alone, and does not indulge in mere exhortation and admonition, but, also by its interpretation of Creation, gives its followers a special outlook and a peculiar way of thinking. And this outlook may be the basis of the Islamic regulations regarding social matters like ownership, government, family rights etc. One of the subjects explained in the Qur'an is that of the creation of man and woman. The importance and value of the views of Islam may be understood when they are compared with others' prates. It has been said in some religious books that woman has been created of some inferior material, and thus she has a parasitic aspect. The

Holy Qur'an, however, explicitly says that God created women of the kind and nature of men: 'He (Allah) made all of you from one being, and from that being He made its mate.' (4:1); and, concerning all human beings, it says: 'He made your mate from among you.' (30:21) Islam has no contemptuous view of woman in regard to her nature and innate character. The Holy Qur'an is opposed to the then prevalent idea according to which 'woman is the cause of all sins. Her very existence stimulates evil. Woman is a little devil. Men themselves are free from sin; it is the women who drag them to it. It is also said that the Devil cannot have direct access to men. It is through women that he lures them. ...' The Qur'an, where it has narrated the story of Paradise, says nowhere that the Devil misled Adam and Eve was responsible for it. It neither blames Eve nor exonerates her. Rather, it puts the pronouns in the dual form and says: 'Then the Satan made a suggestion to them (both). Then he led them (both) on with guile. He swore to them (both): I am a sincere adviser to you (both).' (7:20-21)

The Qur'an has rejected the idea that 'woman could not reach such a stage of proximity to God as man could.' But the Qur'an, in a number of passages, has expressly said that the reward of the Hereafter and the proximity to Allah are not linked with sex. They depend on faith and deeds. If it has mentioned the wives of Noah and Lot as unworthy of their husbands, it has not ignored the wife of the Pharaoh, and has mentioned her as a great woman. Its heroes are both men and women. About Mary (A.S.), it says that she had attained such a high spiritual position that and sublime spiritual position which caused bewilderment even to Zachariah, the Prophet of that period. The only difference Islam maintains between man and woman concerns the matter of the 'journey towards Allah,' in which it regards man more suitable for shouldering the responsibility of Prophethood. But this does not mean man's superiority to woman; that is why we see that Islam has given a higher position to Fāṭimah Zahrā (A.S.) than all her children, who are Imams, and than all prophets except the Holy Prophet (S) who is the seal of prophethood.

Another contemptuous theory that exists about woman is related to renunciation and sacredness of celibacy which has its roots in suspicion about women. Some people consider love for woman to be a great moral evil. Islam is severely opposed to this absurdity. It reckons marriage as sacred and celibacy as dirty. To like woman has been described by Islam as a part of a prophetic character. At the same time, Islam rejected the idea that woman has been created for the benefit of man. The Qur'an expressly says that the earth, the heavens, the air, the clouds, the plants and the animals, all have been created for the sake of mankind. It does not say, however, that woman has been created for the sake of man. According to it, both man and woman have been created for the sake of each other. The Qur'an says:

> They (women) are raiment (comfort, embellishment and protection) for you, and you (men) are raiment for them. (2:187)

Islam rejected the idea that woman is an inescapable evil and a source of misfortune for man. Islam has emphasized that woman is a blessing for man and a source of his comfort and relief. Islam put an end to the idea that 'little significance was attached to the role of woman in childbearing and woman is just as a receptacle for keeping and developing the seed of man' by verses which say 'We have created you from a man and a woman' and some other verses.

Natural Postulates of Family Rights

We have said that man enjoys a sort of innate dignity. The very nature of his creation has bestowed on him a number of inalienable and untransferable rights and freedoms. This is the spirit and basis of the Universal Declaration of Human Rights and Islam supports this spirit. It is evident that the only authoritative source of the knowledge of human rights is the great and valuable book of nature itself and not a body of those few world-dominating people who had a hand in drafting this Declaration. Though they themselves practically may not adhere much to its contents

In our view, natural and inherent rights have arisen from the divine arrangement according to which the creative machinery, keeping in view its aims, is pushing forward all existing things towards that state of perfection, the capability of which is already hidden in their very making. Every natural capability is the basis of one natural right and, at the same time, a natural authority for the implementation of that right. For example, every human child has a right to learn and to go to school, but a lamb has no such rights.

We think that the basis of the family rights should be looked for in nature, like that of all other natural rights. If we look at the natural capabilities of man and woman, we can easily find out whether they should or should not have similar rights and obligations.

The summary of the points about natural postulates of family rights which have been already discussed are as follows:

(1) Natural rights have emerged from the fact that nature has a definite aim and, keeping that aim in view, it has invested all living beings with certain capabilities, and has bestowed on them certain rights.

(2) Man as such enjoys certain rights known as human rights, which are not enjoyed by animals.

(3) To know natural rights and their characteristics, reference should be made to nature itself.

(4) All human beings, as members of a civil society, have equal and similar natural rights, but they differ in regard to acquired rights which depend on their work, accomplishments and participation in the competition of life.

(5) The theory of the similarity of the family rights of man and woman is based on the presumption that the domestic society is just like any civil society. The law of creation has not allotted them different duties and different roles. As for the theory of non-similarity of family rights, it is based on the presumption that the case

of the domestic society is different from that of a civil society. The law of creation has placed them in dissimilar positions, and has visualized a distinct role for each of them. The presumption of similarity of rights of woman and man says that the relations between wife and husband or between parents and children are like relation in a body of individuals, in national and governmental establishments. Such relations do not mean that some individuals inherently have any special position. It is only due to an acquired position that one is a boss and the other is a subordinate. According to the theory of dissimilarity, however, even their natural elementary rights vary. A husband as such has certain rights and obligations and a wife as such has certain other rights and obligations.

As we have already said, to find a theory about the roots of family rights, one has to search in nature; and to do so, he has to take into account capabilities and natural needs of woman and man. There are two views about the social life of man. Some believe that man is social by nature, whereas some others hold that social life is a contractual matter. As far as the domestic life of human beings is concerned, more than one view does not exist. All agree that the domestic life is purely natural. Hence, the case of domestic life is different from social life. Nature has taken measures to the effect that man and certain animals tend, by instinct, to lead a domestic life. There is no historical evidence showing that in some period human beings did not lead a family life. In respect of ownership of property this fact is admitted by all that in the beginning the property was vested in the community and individual ownership was a later development. But that has never been the case with sex. In other words, sociology shows no historical era in which there was not a family system and woman and man had unrestricted sexual relations.

Now, to study and specify the family rights and obligations of man and woman, we should note that whether there are natural differences between woman and man or they are different only in terms of their bodies and if there is some difference, how it influences determination of the rights and obligations of man and woman.

Disparities between Man and Woman

It goes without saying that there are certain differences between woman and man and the wonderful scientific progress of the 20th century has clearly proved the existence of such disparities.

It is amazing that some people insist that the disparity in the physical and psychological capabilities of man and woman is due to the imperfection of woman and the perfection of man. They hold that, for certain good reasons, woman has been intentionally created imperfect. It is still more amazing that some Westerners have lately begun trying to put forward a thousand and one arguments to prove that by creation, man is inferior and imperfect and that woman is superior and perfect. In fact, the differences between man and woman have nothing to do with inferiority or superiority of one of them. The law of creation has decreed that as man and woman have been created to lead a joint life, and these differences are like differences between body limbs difference between which does not mean discrimination. Differences between woman and man are to make them more suitable for each other.

The subject of dissimilarity between man and woman is not a new question, which might have cropped up during our time. It is at least 2,400 year old. Plato in his book *The Republic* expressly maintains that men and women have the same capabilities, and women can perform the same jobs and enjoy the same rights as men do. Plato believes that, like man, woman should also be given military training and, as man takes part in athletic competitions, woman should do so as well. He believes that both man and woman have similar talents. The only thing is that in certain respects woman is weaker than man.

After Plato, his pupil, Aristotle, opposed the views of his teacher in *Politics*. He says that the two sexes have talents of different kinds and, thus, the functions which should be entrusted to them differ greatly. For this reason, their rules of morality are also different in many respects. It is possible that a moral quality may be excellent in regard to man, but it may not be so in regard to woman and vice versa. In the ancient world, the views of Plato were replaced by those of Aristotle. The later intellectuals preferred the views of Aristotle to those of Plato. This was about the ancient world.

The modern world, however, does not resort to speculation and approximation. In the modern world, as the result of deeper medical, psychological and social studies, more and bigger disparities between man and woman, here we mention some of them:

From the physical point of view: Man, on an average has larger limbs and woman smaller. Man is taller and woman is shorter. Man is coarser and woman is finer. Man's voice is comparatively rough and heavy, and woman's delicate and delightful. The bodily growth of woman is quicker, and that of man is slower. Woman reaches the stage of puberty earlier, and loses the capability of reproduction earlier. The average brain of man is larger than the average brain of woman, but, in proportion to the whole body, the average brain of woman is larger.

From the psychological point of view: Psychologically, man is more inclined to physical exercise, hunting and active life. The feelings of man are challenging and bellicose, whereas woman has a peaceful disposition. Man is aggressive; woman is comparatively calm and quiet. Woman avoids violence, and that is why the cases of suicide by women are fewer. Woman is more emotional than man and is more easily excited. Man is comparatively cool-minded. Woman is much interested in ornaments, cosmetics, and make-up. Feelings of woman are not stable. Her feelings are motherly from childhood she cannot compete with man in deductive sciences and dry intellectual subjects, but in literature and arts like painting etc. she is not at all behind him. Man has a greater power of concealing his secrets. He can keep the unhappy happenings to. Good luck from man's point of view means securing a respectable position in the society. But to a woman good luck means to captivate the heart of a man and keep it safe throughout her life.

From the viewpoint of feelings: Man wants to own the woman; woman wants to dominate man's heart. Woman wants man to be courageous and gallant; man wants woman to be beautiful and charming. Woman wants the protection of man. She can control her desires whereas man cannot do so as much as she can. Man's sexual urge is active and aggressive, woman's passive and excitable. Man is a symbol of 'being a lover' and woman is a symbol of 'being beloved'. The purpose of man's feelings is 'to seek and find' and that of woman is 'to be sought and found'.

Irrespective of the question whether or not dissimilarity between man and woman causes the dissimilarity in their respective rights and responsibilities, dissimilarity itself is one of the most wonderful masterpieces of creation. It proves that the system of this world has been most wisely and exquisitely planned. With a view to preserving the species, the great creative mechanism has brought the reproductive system into existence and for that purpose self-interest which is essential to every living being has been converted into sentiments of service, co-operation and tolerance. If woman had the same physical features, the same temperament and the same habits as man has, it would not have been possible for her to attract man towards her. If man had the same physical and psychological features as woman has, she would not have regarded him as her ideal and would not have done anything to win his heart. Man has been created to dominate the world, and woman has been created to dominate man. It is amazing that some individuals cannot differentiate between sexual passion and love. They think that the relation between husband and wife is exclusively based on greed and lust. They interpret the history of man-woman relationship from the angle of employment and exploitation, or on the basis of a struggle for survival! The matrimonial union is something higher than physical passion, and its basis is in what has been described by the Qur'an as 'affection and compassion':

> And of His signs is this that He created your mates from yourselves that you might find rest in them, and He put between you affection and compassion.(30:21)

Study of Islamic Rules Concerning Woman

Now, after speaking of human position of woman in Islam, natural grounds of family rights, differences between woman and man, and the purpose sought by nature through such differences, we will go to discuss our main point to find whether differences maintained by Islamic rules between woman and man according to which they have been placed in different positions are in harmony with the law of creation or not. We claim that principles of family rights in Islam have been postulated according to natural differences between woman and man. Here, we try to find reasons behind legalization of particular Islamic rules in various fields such as suiting, temporary marriage, dower and maintenance, heritage, divorce, and polygamy. The issues which should be still discussed are as follows: man's rule in family, right of custody, term of widowhood and its philosophy, woman and *ijtihād* and *iftā*, woman and judicial and penal rules, morality and education of woman, woman's dress, sexual morality (ardor, chastity, modesty ...), motherhood and woman's working, and some other issues.

Proposal

Proposal is not a straight Islamic Law. Rather, it is based upon precepts that are deduced from general Islamic laws. Some people have objected that proposal of marriage insults woman. And the term of 'taking a wife' shows man as a customer or buyer while the woman is represented as some sort of merchandise. Thus, woman should be able to propose marriage to man. This is one of the great errors which leads to annulment of dower and maintenance which we will discuss later. Contrary to what that these people think that from time immemorial man has approached woman with his proposal and has requested conjugality from her does not insult her, and even this has been the greatest of factors in safe-guarding the prestige and honor of women. As we have already said nature has created man a means of solicitation and woman a source of being loved. Thus, it is contrary to the respect and honor of a woman to run after a man. For a man it is manly that he should approach and solicit a woman for this purpose even if he gets a reply in the negative. In that case he will ask one woman after another until he meets a woman who gives him her consent. For a woman, who aspires to be the object of affection, the beloved, the adored one, to submit to the heart of a man who will govern her existence, it is repugnant for her to invite a man to be her spouse, and, if it happens that her request is turned down, to go in search of another man. William James says that women, in their long history, have learnt that their honor and prestige do not lie in going after a man and in making themselves commonplace, but in keeping themselves aloof beyond the reach of man. The other objection is that this shows man as a buyer of woman. To reply, firstly, we say it is in fact the law of creation that a man runs after a woman. Secondly, a thing desired does not become your property, nor do you become its owner: students are desirous of knowledge, apprentices of crafts desire skillful craftsman. Is it proper that we call those who seek them their owners? Man is desirous of union with woman, not in need of making her his slave. It is the height of her excellence that she can attract man to her wherever he is, and whatever state he is in. Thus, that law is in accord with creation and nature which retains this advantage for women and this obligation on man. Laws based on the similarity of man and woman act against the woman and respect for her and her honor; similarity is seemingly in the interest of man, and works, in fact, against both of them.

Fixed-Time Marriage

One of the glorious laws of Islam, from the point of view of the Ja'farī (Shi'ite) law, is that there are two kinds of marriage, a permanent and a fixed-time marriage. Some of the effects, which flow from these two kinds of marriage, are the same and some others are different. To understand why this rule has been enacted in Islam, we mention some of them:

Dissimilarities: that in a fixed-time marriage, a man and a woman enter into a contract to marry each other for a fixed period, on the expiry of which, if they wish, they can extend it, otherwise they separate. The other distinguishing feature is that there is a greater freedom of choice in fixed-time marriage. For example, in a permanent marriage the husband is bound to maintain his wife and meet her daily expenses, the wife has to accept her husband as the head of the family and obey him within the limits of family interest, but in a fixed-time marriage this also depends on the terms of the contract concluded between two parties. In the case of a permanent marriage wife and husband inherit from each other, but this is not so in a fixed-time marriage. In a permanent marriage neither the husband nor the wife can use any contraceptive methods without the consent of the other, but in the fixed-time marriage such a consent is not necessary.

Similarities: The child born from a fixed-time wedlock is in no way legally different from the child born as a result of a permanent marriage. 'Dower' is necessary, both in the case of a permanent and a fixed-time marriage, with the only difference that the non-specification of dower at the time of marriage makes the fixed-time marriage void, but does not affect the validity of permanent marriage. In a permanent marriage, the husband is debarred from ever marrying the mother or daughter of the wife and the wife is permanently debarred from marrying the father or son of the husband. Similar is the case with regard to fixed time marriage. To have two sisters as wives at the same time is prohibited both in the case of a permanent as well a fixed-time marriage. As it is forbidden to propose to a permanently married woman, similarly, it is not allowed to give an offer of marriage to a woman who is married under fixed-time marriage rules. As adultery with the permanent wife of someone else permanently debars a person from marrying her, the same restriction is imposed in the case of adultery with the fixed-time wife of someone else. After getting a divorce, just as the permanent wife has to pass through a period of probation, the fixed-time wife also has to pass a period of probation. The only difference is that in the case of a permanent wife the *'iddah* is three monthly periods, whereas in the case of a fixed-time wife it is two periods or 45 days.

This is what is meant by a fixed-time marriage, according to the Shi'ite law. Obviously we support this law with the prescribed conditions and specifications. If some people misused it in the past or are still misusing it, that has nothing to do with the legal system as such. The abolition of this law can serve no useful purpose, as, with its abolition, malpractices will not stop, but will only take a different shape. Moreover, the abolition of this law will give rise to many other evils. Now let us see why it is necessary to have the institution of a fixed-time marriage side by side with that of a permanent marriage. If a fixed-time marriage is necessary, is it compatible with the present day conditions and modern-ideas of human values?

Benefits of Fixed-Time Marriage

There are many social and moral benefits with fixed-time marriage and, here, we mention some of them:

1. As we learnt previously, a permanent marriage imposes heavy responsibilities and obligations both on husband and wife. The requirements of the modern age have lengthened the interval between natural puberty and social maturity, when one is capable of building a family. In ancient times, a boy could, from his age of early puberty, undertake a job which he continued to practice till the last days of his life. But nowadays that is no longer possible. Nowadays, if you ask a 18-year-old boy or a 16 years old girl, whose sexual urge is at its height, to marry, the people will laugh at you.

Now, how can we react to nature and sexual instinct? Is nature prepared to delay puberty or the sexual urge since the conditions of life in the present world do not allow us to marry at the age of 16 or 18? Are our young men prepared to pass a period of temporary monasticism and live a life of renunciation and extreme austerity, till they become eligible for a permanent marriage? Even if a young man is willing to accept the life of temporary hermitage, is nature prepared to excuse him from the tensions and nervous disorders which usually result from abstaining from normal sexual activity? The other way is to let a young boy enjoy hundreds of girls, and a young girl to have illicit relations with many boys, and then undergo several abortions. And in this case, will it ever be possible for these boys and girls, who have had unlimited affairs during the period of their studies, to lead a normal domestic life? Of course, no. Thus, the only way is a fixed-time marriage which restricts woman to have only one husband at one time. It is obvious that a limitation of woman means a limitation of man also. Thus boys and girls can pass through their period of studies without facing the ill effects of temporary hermitage, or of falling into the abyss of sexual communism.

2. In principle it is possible for man and woman, who intend to marry on permanent basis but could not achieve full confidence in each other, to get married on trial for a temporary period. If they have developed sufficient trust they continue their marital position, otherwise they separate from each other.

3. Fixed-time marriage helps to protect the family system in the society. The reason that westerners think that there should be some prostitutes in certain places in every city who work under governmental supervision is that presence of single men who are not able to marry threatens foundations of families. Today, we see that some western thinkers such as Russell and Lindsay ... propose companionship marriage which is a little

different from the Islamic fixed-time marriage, but this suggestion indicates that thinkers of their caliber have realized that a normal permanent marriage does not meet all the needs of the society.

Objections against fixed-time marriage: Everything has been said about a fixed-time marriage, but what really constitutes the spirit of this law has been left out.

Had it been a Western gift the position would have been quite different. Here, we pose these objections and provide replies for them:

(1) The basis of marriage must be permanent. From the beginning of conjugal relations, husband and wife should know that they permanently belong to each other. The idea of a separation must not enter into their minds. The fixed-time marriage does not constitute a permanent contract between husband and wife. It is true that the basis of marriage should be permanent. However, this objection can be valid only if we oppose a permanent marriage and wish to replace it by a fixed-time marriage. The law of fixed-time marriage has been laid down only because a permanent marriage alone cannot meet all the human requirements in all circumstances.

(2) Iranian women and girls, in spite of being *Shī'ah*, have not welcomed the idea of fixed-time marriage. They regard it as a sort of insult to them. Hence, the general opinion among the *Shī'ah* has also rejected it.

It may be said in reply that *Shī'ah* woman hate fixed-time marriage because of misuses made by the licentious men. It is the duty of the government to prevent its misuse. Secondly, it is unreasonable to expect a fixed-time marriage to be as popular as a permanent marriage, because the former is meant only to satisfy the needs of the parties concerned, if both are or at least one of them is unable or unwilling to contract a permanent marriage.

(3) A fixed-time marriage amounts to the hiring of a human body. It is against the self-respect of a woman to put herself at the disposal of any man in exchange for money.

Firstly a fixed-time marriage, as described above by us, has not the remotest connection with sale or hire. Can it become sale or hire simply because the duration of wedlock is limited? Jurists are unanimous that, with regard to the nature of a contract, there is no difference between a permanent and a fixed-time marriage. They are two forms of marriage and their contracts can be constituted only by using a specific formula (*sīghah* relating to marriage). If a contract of a fixed-time marriage is expressed in the form of sale or hire, it is invalid.

Secondly, since when has the practice of hiring human beings been abolished? All the tailors, barbers, cooks, and all the factory workers are hired men. Thirdly, is a woman, who, by her own free will, contracts a fixed-time marriage with a particular man a hired woman and does not do anything derogatory to her self-respect or human dignity? Or, is it that European woman who, to earn money, gives her body, soul, and personality to film companies, cabarets, hotels, hypermarkets, and other economic firms, to trap more clients for them?

(4) After all, a fixed-time marriage legalizes polygamy, which is an abominable practice. Hence a fixed-time marriage is condemnable. As far as polygamy is concerned, we shall discuss it later in details.

(5) As a fixed-time marriage has no permanency, it leaves the future children shelterless. They become nobody's responsibility. They are deprived of a father's protection and a mother's affection.

We have previously said that one of the differences between a temporary and a permanent marriage is that, firstly, in a permanent marriage neither of the spouses can evade the responsibility of begetting children, but, in a fixed-time marriage, both the parties are free. Thus, in the case of a fixed-time marriage, if both the husband and wife are inclined, they can beget children, provided they accept the responsibility of rearing them. It is obvious that, from the standpoint of natural affection, there is no difference between the child of a permanent wife and that of a fixed-time one. Should a father or a mother abstain from performing his or her duty, it is the responsibility of the law to compel them in the same way as it intervenes in the case of divorce.

6- It is alleged that the legality of a fixed-time marriage is equivalent to the legality of a *'ḥarem'* formation. It is equivalent to the legalization of licentiousness, every form of which is contrary to morality and causes decline and ruin.

(1) What were the social factors which led to a *'harem'* formation in the past and whether the law of fixed-time marriage influenced this phenomenon?

(2) Does the law of a fixed-time marriage aim at providing an opportunity of *'harem'* formation to the licentious men?

Thus, the above issue should be discussed from these two angles:

Social Causes of *'Harem'* Formation

There were two factors which brought *'harems'* into existence. The first was the piety and chastity of woman. In other words, a *'harem'* can be formed only in an atmosphere where social and moral conditions are such that a woman is not allowed to have sexual relations with more than one man. In such circumstances a licentious man has no alternative but to gather together a number of women and form a *harem*. Obviously, in an atmosphere where importance is not attached to chastity and women are available easily and freely, nobody will take the trouble of forming a big *'harem'* at a huge cost and with a large paraphernalia. The second factor was the non-existence of social justice. The atmosphere conducive to *'harem'* formation is that in which a few are steeped in all sorts of luxuries and affluence, whereas others are unable to make both ends meet, and in which there are many who are unable to have a wife and form a family. In such an atmosphere the number of unmarried women grows and a suitable ground for a *'harem'* formation is furnished. If social justice is established and the means of forming a family and choosing a spouse are available to all, automatically every eligible woman becomes attached to one particular man and no opportunity is left for debauchery, licentiousness and *'harem'* formation. It is customary that history narrates the stories of the *'harems'* of the caliphs and the sultans and describes the pomp and show of their courts, but ignores to explain the privation, misery and sufferings of those whom the social conditions did not allow to have spouses. A cursory glance over history shows that the law of fixed-time marriage has not exercised even the slightest influence over *'harem'* formation. None of the Abbasid Caliphs and the Ottoman Sultans, who were famous for keeping large *'harems,'* was a follower of the *Shī'ah* theology, and so none of them could be expected to have taken advantage of the law of fixed-time marriage. The *Shī'ah* Sultans never vied in this respect with the Abbasid Caliphs or the Ottoman Sultans. This clearly shows that the *'harems'* were the outcome of some other special social factors.

Has Fixed-Time Marriage Been Made Lawful to Satisfy Lust?

There are no two opinions about the fact that heavenly religions, on the whole, censure licentiousness and immorality, so much so that the followers of most of them have preferred a life of renunciation and asceticism. One of the clear and accepted principles of Islam is to combat lewdness, which has been compared to idolatry by the Qur'an . Islam has described a 'taster', i.e. a man who wants to enjoy various types of women, as condemned and hated by Allah. One of the distinctive features of Islam is that it rejects monkery and renunciation, but does not allow lewdness. According to Islam, all natural desires should be satisfied within natural limits. The modern world has apparently made *'ḥarems'* obsolete. One of the two factors which brought it into existence has been removed. But which factor? Not that of the social inequality, but it is that of the piety and chastity of woman which has been removed. The lewd man of this century is no longer in need of taking the trouble of forming a *'ḥarem'* and of bearing the huge expenses of maintaining it. It should be noted here that other Muslim schools of theology do not allow fixed-time marriage.

All the Muslims are unanimous that during the early period of Islam fixed-time marriage was permissible and the Holy Prophet(S) and the second caliph, during the period of his caliphate, banned it. The correct explanation of this point is that which has been given by 'Allāmah Kāshif al-Ghiṭā. The caliph banned temporary marriage, because he thought that the matter was within his constitutional power as Head of the State. In other words, the caliph's order was political and not legal. The caliph intended to prevent the dispersal of the companions of the Prophet in the newly acquired territories and their mixing with the newly converted Muslims. Obviously, this was a temporary consideration. But later, when the life of the early caliphs came to be regarded as a model, their orders assumed the form of a permanent law. It was in these circumstances that, with a view to ensuring that this Islamic tradition might not be completely forgotten, the Imāms, who are the defenders of the faith, encouraged it and vehemently pleaded for it. It seems that, when the Imāms forbade men having a wife to contract a fixed-time marriage, they wanted to make it clear that it was not meant for those who were not in need of it.

Guidance and encouragement for general public to take somebody in fixed-time marriage is an important step towards 'revival of abandoned custom' or tradition. Anyway it is a definite fact that the meaning and intention of the first legislator on promotion and explanation of this law and the purpose of the infallible Imāms to encourage it on those lines was never to have such provision exist as a means towards sexual adventures, evil desires and build-up of *harems* for beastly human beings nor to victimize helpless and oppressed women and orphaned children.

Woman and Social Independence

One of the other objections posed against Islam is that it is against woman's social independence; for it is father who is absolutely competent to make decision for his daughter. A girl who has gone to university and attained high scientific position, even if she is 30 or 40 years old, cannot marry without permission of her father or grandfather, even if he illiterate.

Here, again, we emphasize that mistakes committed by people should not be regarded as being stemmed from Islamic progressive laws. If we look at the pre-Islamic history, we find that Islam has made the greatest services to women. Authorities of fathers had been so extended that they gave their still-uborn daughters in marriage to other men and when their daughters were born and came to the age of puberty, those men were entitled to take those girls. *Shighār* marriage (exchange of daughters) was a manifestation of the absolute authority of the fathers. A man would give his daughter in marriage to another man in consideration of the latter giving his daughter in marriage to him. In such a form of marriage each of women was the dower of the other. Islam abolished this custom, and rejected fathers' absolute authority; and, in general, Islam not only put an end to the absolute control of the fathers, but gave women freedom, a personality and independence of thinking and opinion.. It is worth noting that the Holy Prophet (S) allowed full liberty to his daughter Fāṭimah Zahrā (A.S.) in choosing her husband. And, she rejected some of her suitors.

However, there are two basic differences between the steps taken by Islam and what is happening in the West: The first difference concerns the psychology of man and woman which we have already discussed in details. The second difference is that, while Islam made the women aware of their rights and gave them an identity, a personality, freedom and independence, it did not instigate them to revolt and harbor malice against the male persons. It did not put an end to the respect in which the daughters held their fathers and the wives their husbands. It did not upset the basis of the family life and did not make women suspicious of their responsibilities in regard to their fathers and husbands. It did not snatch away the wives from their husbands and the daughters from their parents and did not hand them over to the sensual executives and the moneyed magnates.

The question, which needs examination from the point of view of the authority exercised by fathers over their daughters, is whether the father's consent is essential in the case of a maiden's first marriage. From the Islamic point of view certain things are indisputable. According to Islam, the boy and the girl both are economically independent. Every sane adult is entitled to have full control of his or her property, provided he or she is mentally mature, that is, capable of taking care of themselves. And nobody has power of supervision or intervention in this respect. The adult and mature boys have full liberty in marriage and nobody else has any right of intervention. The position of the girl, who has been married once and is now without a husband, is the same. But the case of a maiden, who wants to marry for the first time, is a little different. It is beyond any doubt that the father cannot force even a maiden to marry any person against her will. There is one more point about which there is absolutely no dispute. If the father withholds his consent without a sound reason, he loses his right. The only point the jurists differ on it is that whether the validity of the marriage of a maiden depends on the consent of her father. Most of the jurists are of the view that it does not. But still there are some who are of the opinion that it does. This being a disputed point, it is not possible to discuss it from the Islamic point of view. The basis of the rule that the maidens must not or, at least, should not marry without the consent of their fathers is not that they are considered to be less mature than the boys. Had it been so, there should have been no difference between a 16 year old girl, who had previously been married, and as such does not require her father's consent, and an 18 year old maiden who requires it according to the view of some jurists. Moreover, had Islam considered girls to be immature it would not have regarded the transactions, involving money and properties, made by them independently, as valid. It is not a question of the immaturity or intellectual inadequacy of woman. It is related to a definite aspect of the psychology of the two sexes. As we previously said, man is after sex and woman is after love. Man is overpowered by his sexual urge; it is, however, the melody of love, sincerity and faithfulness which subdues woman. As long as the woman is a maiden and has had no experience of men, she can easily be lured by his love songs. That is why it is essential that a girl, who has had no experience of men, should consult her father and should obtain his consent. The law has in no way degraded woman, but has taken a step to protect her.

Dower and Maintenance

It is one of the most ancient traditions of the human family relations that at the time of marriage the man pays a dower (*mahr*) to the woman or to her father. In addition to that, he undertakes to bear the expenses of his wife and children during the entire period of his life. Though Islam abolished many pre-Islamic customs and usages in connection with dower, it kept its basis. And because of this, some objections were posed against Islam. Critics say: 'As one has to spend money for getting a garden, a house, a horse or a mule, similarly money has to be spent to purchase a woman. And as the price of a house, a garden or a horse depends upon its size, beauty and usefulness, similarly the price of a woman varies according to her beauty or ugliness and her wealth or poverty. If economic equality between man and woman is established, there is no reason to specify dower and maintenance for her. But as man has the right of divorce and woman has no guarantee of the continuity of a joint life with him, she is given a right to demand a sort of security from him. In case man does not have an absolute right of divorce, no justification is left for the continuation of the custom of dower. On the other hand, it is not clear why, in the period of abstention for husband' death when woman needs to be soothed and her subsistence should be provided, no maintenance is provided for her. Anyway, dower and maintenance are remnants of the days when man owned woman and justice and the equality of rights demand that these outdated traditions should be abolished, a marriage should take place without a dower, woman should be responsible to bear her own expenses, and the children should be the joint responsibility of husband and wife.'

We propose to answer these questions, and begin with the question of dower. Let us see how this tradition came into being, what its philosophy is and how the sociologists explain its origin. It is said that during pre-historic times man lived a barbaric life, which had the tribal form. At that time ancestry was traced through the mothers. Men were considered to be barren and sterile. It was not long before man discovered his role in procreation and came to believe that the children in reality belonged to him. From then onwards, he dominated over woman and the so called period of patriarchy began. During this period also a marriage between the people having the same blood was prohibited. Man had to choose his wife from some other tribe, and bring her to his own tribe. As there was constant warfare among the tribes, the only way to get a wife was to kidnap a young girl from some other tribe. Gradually peace took the place of warfare and the different tribes were able to achieve peaceful coexistence. During this period the custom of kidnapping the girls was abolished. In order to get the girl of his choice the man went to her tribe, became a hired worker of her father and worked for him for some time. In consideration of the services rendered by him the girl's father gave her hand to him and he took her to his own tribe. When money became common, man discovered that instead of serving the bride's father for years, it was better to present a suitable gift to him and take the girl immediately. That was the origin of the dower (*mahr*). Since the time man laid the foundation of patriarchy, he gave woman the status of a slave, or at the most, of an employee or a servant of his. He looked upon her as an economic tool, which, by the way, could satisfy his lust also. The money which man paid as dower and the expenses which he bore as maintenance (*nafaqah*) were in consideration of the economic gains which he derived from her during the period of conjugal relations.'

There is a fifth stage also about which the sociologists and other commentators have observed silence. During this stage man gives a present to woman herself. Neither of her parents has any claim to it. Woman receives the present, but she preserves her social and economic independence. She chooses her husband of her own free will. Furthermore, neither has her father nor her husband any right to enslave or exploit her. In financial matters she does not require anybody's supervision or patronage. The husband has only one right. He can enjoy sex with his wife. As long as the conjugal relations are intact, he is under obligation to meet all the legitimate requirements of his wife within his own financial limits. This is the stage which is recognized by Islam.

To be able to grasp the philosophy of the dower and maintenance in the fifth stage and to reply objections posed about dower and maintenance in Islam, we should examine the theory of the four periods mentioned above. The fact is that all that is said about these periods is nothing more than a hypothesis based on presumptions and speculations. it neither constitutes a historical fact nor a scientific truth. There are two things which strike one's mind about these presumptions and speculations. One is that the primitive man has been represented to be extraordinarily barbarous, violent and devoid of human sentiments. The second thing is that the wonderful planning of nature, to reach its universal goals has been ignored.

According to our belief, the dower has come into being as the result of skilful arrangements, put into the very design of creation, to balance the relations between man and woman. We have already pointed out that feelings and sentiments of woman and man, with regard to each other, are not the same. The law of creation has ordained that woman should have the qualities of beauty, pride and indifference, whereas man should have those of courting and pursuit. That is how the physical weakness of woman, as compared to man, has been counterbalanced. That man is more lustful than woman and woman has a better sense of self-restraint has enabled her not to run after man, nor to submit to him easily. Man's instinct compels him to approach woman, and he takes steps to gain her favor. One of these steps is to present her with a gift. She knows by instinct that her self-respect demands that she should not submit herself freely. That is how woman, in spite of her physical weakness, has been able to bring men to their knees, to compel them to vie with each other. When she agrees to marry a man, she receives a present from him as a sign of cordiality. That faculty of woman has enabled her to inspire man to love to perform feats of bravery; to excel in intellectual and creative deeds. Hence, this tendency has impelled bridegroom to offer his bride a present at the time of marriage as the dower. The form of the dower is not an invention of the Qur'an . All that the Qur'an did was to restore it to its natural form. The Qur'an says: 'Give to the women a free gift of their marriage portions.' In this short sentence the Holy Qur'an has referred to three basic points: Firstly it has used for marriage portion or the dower the word, *ṣaduqātehinna* meaning truthfulness and sincerity and not the word *mahr*. Secondly, it is clear from the above verse of the Qur'an that the dower is to be paid directly to the woman, and her parents have no claim to it. It is not a compensation for the efforts made by them to bring up their daughter. Thirdly, it is clear that the dower is nothing except a present and a gift.

The law of sexuality is not confined to human beings. It prevails in the animal kingdom also. Though both the sexes are in need of each other, the male feels a greater need for the female, and takes the initiative in gaining her favor. That is why the male does not misuse his superior strength, and assumes a meek attitude towards the female. In the West, where in the name of equality of human rights, an attempt is being made to allot man and woman similar functions in domestic life and nullify dower and maintenance, man still performs his natural role, as far as free love is concerned. In free love he still offers presents to woman and bears her expenses, even in this case woman feels it as an insult to bear expenses of man. This means that European love-making is more natural than European marriage.

So far, we have described the philosophy and origin of dower. It was also pointed out that the custom of dower has originated from the gentle and affectionate feelings of man, and not from his sense of domination and harshness. The role played by woman in this connection has proceeded from her peculiar sense of self-restraint, and not from any weakness or helplessness on her part. Here we mention some of the customs of pre-Islamic era which Islam abolished:

During the pre-Islamic period the parents thought that

dower belonged to them exclusively as a recompense for the pains they took in rearing and bringing up the girl. When a girl was born and somebody wanted to congratulate her father, he did so by saying: 'May this musk-bag be beneficial to you.' What he meant was: 'May you give her in marriage and receive her dower.' During the pre-Islamic period, the fathers and, in their absence, the brothers, as natural guardians of the girl, gave her in marriage according to their own will. At the same time they regarded her dower as belonging to themselves. They sometimes exchanged their daughters and took each one of them as the dower of the other (*Shighār* marriage). According to the Islamic traditions not only a father has no claim to any part of the dower of his daughter, but it is also not permissible to include, in the marriage agreement, a condition that apart from dower anything additional would be paid to him. Islam also abolished the custom according to which a man worked for his prospective father-in-law.

During the pre-Islamic period there existed other customs also, which practically deprived the woman of her dower. One of them was the custom of inheriting conjugal rights. If a man died, his son or brother inherited his conjugal rights, in respect of his wife, in the same way as he inherited his property. The son or the brother of the deceased had a right, either to give the widow in marriage to another man and take her dower, or to declare her his own wife without paying a dower. The Holy Qur'an did away with this custom also. It says: 'O you who believe! It is not lawful for you to inherit women forcibly.' (4:19) In another verse, the holy Qur'an has totally banned a marriage with one's father's wife (stepmother) even if she be willing. It says: 'Marry not those women whom your father married.' (4:22) The Holy Qur'an did away with every custom which deprived woman of her dower. One of such customs was that when a man lost interest in his wife, he harassed her with a view to making her agree to a divorce on the condition that she would return, wholly or partly, the dower which she had received. The Holy Qur'an says: 'Nor should you put constraint on them (women) so that you take away part of what you have given.'(4:19) Another obnoxious custom was that a man would marry a woman and even pay her heavy dower, but after losing interest in her he would tarnish her image, accuse her of adultery and demand the dower back. This custom was also done away with by the Holy Qur'an.

The Holy Qur'an considers the gift given by man to woman as something naturally necessary and says that woman's role is to respond to man's love. It is good if she loves a man but her love should be a reaction to the initiative taken by him. If she falls in love with a man who already does not want her, she would invariably be faced with failure and this will strike a blow to her personality. Is it true that woman is not consistent in love? If she is first to fall in love, such a love is not reliable. But it is false if woman's love is in response to man's sincere love.

Now, the objections posed by critics may be replied as follows: A dower is neither a price for woman nor a right of ownership for man. It is still more baseless to describe dower as a financial security against the right of divorce. Furthermore, this statement means that when the Holy Prophet (S) fixed the dower of his own wives, he provided them with a security against himself. Similarly, when he fixed the dower of Lady Fāṭimah at the time of her marriage with Imām 'Alī, he did so because he wanted to provide the former with a security against the latter. Why did the Holy Prophet (S) counsel the women to consent formally to surrender their dower to their husbands? Why did he advise that, as far as possible, the amount of dower should not be large? Does not all this show that the Prophet considered dower to be a gift and regarded its voluntary surrender as a means of strengthening and consolidating love between a husband and a wife? Why did the Qur'an say: 'Give the women their dower as a free gift'; and why did it not say: 'Give the women their dower as a security?' Furthermore, it appears that the critic is under the impression that, in the early days of Islam, dower had the same form as it has today. At present, the common practice is that the husband, at the time of marriage, undertakes to pay a certain amount. But, during the early Islamic period, the usual practice was to make a prompt payment of the amount promised. And dower was not confined to cash; for example, sometimes, teaching the Holy Qur'an was taken as dower.

DOWER AND MAINTENANCE

We have mentioned the Islamic point of view regarding dower and its philosophy. Now let us take up the question of maintenance. Before going to discuss maintenance in Islam, it is useful to mention that, until recent times, in the western world, was interdicted from entering into any transaction in respect of her property. In the 19th Century, the first laws of woman's economic independence vis-a-vis her husband were enacted and the so-called ban on married woman was removed. And in the 20th Century, ban on all women was removed. Was the human conscience suddenly awakened and they thus realized the injustice of their ways? No, but as Will Durant says the European woman should in fact be thankful for her emancipation and for acquiring proprietary rights by her to the machines and not to any man. She should bow her head in reverence for the enactment and gratitude of the law of economic independence by the British Parliament, and not to the industrialists, who wanted to earn more profits and pay less wages.

We see, however, that Islam, 1400 years ago (almost 13 centuries before Europe), laid down the following law of economic independence for woman and man:

> 'Men have a portion of what they have earned and women have a portion of what they have earned.' (4:32)

The differences are as follows:

(1) The considerations which motivated Islam were purely human, moral and divine. There did not exist any such motives as the greed of the mill-owners;

(2) Islam gave equal rights to woman, but did not disrupt the basis of her domestic life, nor did it instigate the wives and daughters to revolt against their husbands and fathers.

(3) The Western world did was to save woman from the drudgery of household work and to foist on her the drudgery in stores and factories. According to the Islamic point of view, she has every right to earn money, to keep it safe and to develop her wealth, but at the same time she should not be put under the pressure of the compulsions of life.

May we ask the critic how she has come to the conclusion that a husband owns his wife or that ownership is the reason why her maintenance has been made obligatory on him. What sort of ownership is this that the master cannot even ask his bondsmaid to give him a glass of water? What sort of ownership is this that whatever the bondsmaid earns belongs to her and not to her master? What sort of ownership is this that the bondsmaid can, if she likes, ask for wages for the slightest service done by her to her master? What sort of ownership is this that the master has no right to force his bondsmaid even to suckle his child?

Secondly it is amazing that some people say: why is not maintenance obligatory in the period of abstention after death of husband, while in this period woman is more in need? It seems that they live in the 19th Century Europe where woman had no right of ownership and immediately after husband's death she became helpless. When Islam has granted the right of ownership to woman and, since her living is provided by husband, whey should there be maintenance after husband's death? Maintenance is woman's right for embellishing man's home, and when this home is destructed, maintenance will be no more necessary.

Secondly, is each and every one who receives maintenance owned by the other? Islam recognizes three kinds of maintenance.

(1) The person who owns animals has to maintain them. The basis of this kind of maintenance is ownership.

(2) Man has to bear the expenses of his children, if they are minors or if they are poor. Similarly, one has to maintain one's parents if they are poor. The basis of this kind of maintenance is not ownership. It is based on natural rights. This kind of maintenance is conditional on need.

(3) A husband has to maintain his wife. The basis of this kind of maintenance is neither ownership nor any natural right in the above mentioned sense. Nor is it conditional on any need, pecuniary or otherwise. Another distinctive feature of this kind of maintenance is that, unlike the first two kinds, it is judicially enforceable.

Islam, in an unprecedented manner, has safeguarded the economic and financial interests of woman. Now, we will go to find what the condition of this kind of maintenance is and why Islam has taken off from woman's shoulders any responsibility to meet family expenses.

The truth is that Islam has intended neither to favor man nor to favor woman. Islam is not partial to either of them. It has not only aimed at the welfare of both man and woman, but also of their prospective children and the entire humanity. Islam has always kept this fact in view that man is a symbol of need, desire and pursuit and woman is a symbol of indifference. From the Islamic point of view, in union and in family life, man should consider himself to be a beneficiary and should be prepared to bear her necessary expenditure.

Another reason why the husband has been made responsible for maintaining his wife is that it is she who suffers all the pains in connection with child-bearing. Man's natural role in this respect is only momentary and pleasure-giving. It is the woman who has to bear all the troubles connected with pregnancy, delivery, suckling and nursing the child. All these functions consume her energy and reduce her working capacity. If it is decided that the law will give no protection to woman and will put both man and woman on an equal footing with regard to contributing to the family budget, the position of woman would no doubt become unenviable. Among those animals also which live in pairs, the male always protects the female and helps her during breeding in securing food.

Furthermore, from the viewpoint of the working capacity and the ability to perform hard and rough and productive and economic jobs, man and woman are not equal, while woman needs more money than man. Her tendency to beautification has created in her a longing for variety and diversity and this requires much more money which woman is not able to earn by herself. Woman's womanhood, that is her beauty, vivacity and pride, demand more comfort and less effort. Obviously, a woman who is not mentally satisfied can neither look after herself properly nor can she be a source of delight to her husband. This is the very reason why men are prepared to put their hard-earned money willingly at the disposal of their wives. In the division of labor in the family life, it is man who is more suited to take part in the struggle of life and woman is more suited to play the role of a comforter. If woman wants to live as magnificently as she desires, she must get the support of her legal husband. Otherwise, she will have to depend upon other men. That is why the lustful men and sex perverts make so much propaganda against the maintenance of the wife by the husband. Of course, the idea of the abolition of this system finds support from those men also who are fed up with the extravagance of their wives.

Some people in modern Europe, in their advocacy of woman's liberation, have gone to the extent of supporting the restoration of the matriarchal system and exclusion of father from the family! At the same time, these people call on the government to take the place of the father and give a subsidy to the women who are unwilling to shoulder the responsibility of forming a family alone, so that they may not stop bearing children and the human race may not come to an end! In other words, woman, who, so far, was a dependent and, according to some critics, a bondsmaid of man, will in future become a dependent and bondsmaid of the government. In reply, it should be said that abolition of payment of maintenance by father weakens motherhood feelings and emotions and, at the same time, changes motherhood from an emotional process to a labor. Under such circumstances, everything may be obtained unless happiness and spiritual pleasures which can be enjoyed in family life.

Anyway, we wanted to say that even the advocates of full independence of woman think that woman's natural contribution in reproduction creates some right which, according to them, the government has to compensate. Even we see that in the labor laws of the world as well as in the Declaration of Human Rights, the minimum remuneration considered for a man should cover his expenses as well as those of his family. In other words, they recognize the right of maintenance for his wife and children. Thus, neither Islam nor Declaration of Human Rights regard maintenance as derogatory to woman. Rather, they have taken into account the fact that woman is financially in need to man and man is a relying point for woman.

Inheritance

In the ancient world woman inherited nothing and, even when she inherited, she was treated like a minor. She had no independent legal personality. According to certain ancient legal systems, a daughter received an inheritance but her children did not. On the other hand, a son not only received an inheritance himself, but his children also inherited the property left by their grandfather. Certain other legal systems allowed a progenitor to make a bequest in her favor. The main reason of the deprivation of woman of inheritance was the prevention of transfer of wealth from one family to another. According to the old belief, the women's role in procreation was insignificant. On this account, they believed that the children of a man's son were his own children and a part of his family, but the children of a man's daughter were not a part of his family, for they were a part of the family of their paternal grandfather. The exclusion of woman from inheritance had other reasons also, one of them being that she was not fit to be a good soldier. We see that the in the pre-Islamic era, Arabs said that a woman was unable to carry arms and to fight the enemy. It was the men who defended themselves and the women. Hence, they alone had the right to inherit the property. The pre-Islamic Arabs sometimes adopted someone as their son. The adopted son, being considered to be just like a real son, enjoyed such privileges as were not allowed to the lineal daughters.

Another custom, which was common among the pre-Islamic Arabs was that of alliance. Two persons unrelated to each other, used to enter into an alliance according to which they defended each other during their lifetime, and whosoever died first the other took his property. In addition, sometimes, the widow of deceased husband was regarded as a part of inheritance, which was discussed under 'Dower and Maintenance'. In Iran, during Sassanid age, women were not under better circumstances. After being married, a girl was not entitled to receive any inheritance from her father. And, in some kinds of marriage, daughters of some wives of a man were not entitled to receive any inheritance.

The Islamic law of inheritance is free from all the shortcomings and defects of the past. The only thing, which is objectionable in the eyes of the upholders of equality between man and woman, is that the share of woman is half that of man. They assert that, after all, there is no necessity of lessening woman's share in inheritance and compensating her for the loss by allowing her dower and maintenance. In reply, we say that firstly the dower and the maintenance are the effects of women's peculiar position with regard to inheritance, whereas the real position is just the reverse. Secondly, in Islam the financial aspect is not the only consideration. The reason why Islam has specified the share of woman half that of man is particular situation of woman according to some penal laws.

As we have already said, woman's earning capacity is less than that of man and, on the other hand, her consumption of wealth is more. In addition, there are several other finer aspects of their respective mental make-up. For example, man always wants to spend for the sake of the woman of his choice. Other psychological and social aspects, which help in the consolidation of the domestic relations, have also been considered. Taking all these points into consideration, Islam has made dower and maintenance obligatory. Such obligations have indirectly imposed a burden on man's budget to compensate it, Islam has specified man's share twice that of man. Such an objection was posed in the time of Imām Ja'far al-Ṣādiq (A.S.) by Ibn Abī al-'Awjā. To reply, Imām says it is so, because woman is exempted from performing military service. Further, Islam had enjoined upon man to pay her dower and maintenance and, in certain criminal cases where the kinsmen of the offender have to contribute to the blood-money, she is exempted from such payment. These were the reasons why her share had been reduced.

Divorce

In no age other than ours has the danger of the disintegration of the family and its harmful consequences so attacked us. In spite of many attempts to prevent this disease, it is again seen that, despite of attempts made by legislators, lawyers, psychologists ... to consolidate marriages, cases of divorce are increasing. In the past much attention was not paid to the problem of divorce, its causes and its harmful effects, nor were any measures devised to prevent its incidence, yet the cases of divorce were few and far between. There is no doubt that the difference between the past and the present is due to the fact that social life has taken such a turn that now there are more chances of the disruption of the family bond.

The western journalists have admitted that the cause of many divorces is not disagreement between wife and husband, but their disinterest in being restrained by domestic bond and interest in enjoying more pleasures is the main cause. Pleasure-seeking has been preferred over faithfulness to family, and this has been caused by licentiousness in the western society. Restaurants, magazines, books ... show naked women and, in this way, provoke sexual problems and weaken the foundations of the family system. Divorce is one of the evil effects of licentiousness. Thus, if the western woman has lost her balance and gives preference to pleasure-seeking over faithfulness to her husband and family she is not to blame. It is the social atmosphere which has struck at the very root of the family system.

Some Theories about Divorce

Now let us see whether, in principle, divorce is good or bad. The question is whether it is good to keep the door to divorce wide open. Who should exercise the right of divorce, should only man or only woman, or both? In the last alternative, how? Should man and woman have the same procedure or should each sex have a separate procedure? In all, these are the five theories in respect of divorce:

(1) Free divorce without any legal or moral restriction. There are those who look at marriage only from a viewpoint of pleasure-seeking; who attach no sanctity to it; and who do not take into consideration the social value of home and family. In this theory not only has the social value of the family been forgotten, but also the delight and satisfaction, which the stability of a conjugal union affords, has been ignored. This theory is so puerile and immature that needs not to be discussed.

(2) Marriage is a sacred undertaking. This is the same theory, which for centuries has been advocated by the Catholic Church, and is still being advocated. The supporters of this theory are on the decrease in the world. Now only Italy and the Catholic Spain adhere to it. Marriage in Italy means bondage for woman. Owing to the non-existence of divorce, many people in Italy have to

resort to unlawful sexual relations. Many of Italians have renounced their Italian nationality for that very reason. We believe that marriage is a sacred bond and it should be lasting and durable. But it can last only as long as both the spouses co-operate with each other. There are situations when a mutual understanding between a wife and her husband is not possible. In such circumstances the forces of law cannot be used to keep them attached to each other in the name of a conjugal bond. The theory of the Church has been a complete failure.

(3) Marriage is dissoluble only by man. In the ancient world many people held such a view and some unfair people assign it Islam, while Islam is free of such ideas and we will explain this point later. But now we do not think it has any supporters. So we need not discuss it also.

(4) Marriage is a sacred institution and the domestic system is respectable, but the way to divorce, with certain conditions, should be open to both the spouses and the procedure of dissolving a marriage should be the same for both of them. Otherwise, there would be a discrimination. We will discuss this theory and reveal its defects in details.

(5) No doubt the marriage institution is sacred, the domestic system is respectable, divorce is abominable and it is an essential duty of society to remove the causes which lead to divorce, yet divorce cannot be totally banned and the way out of a deadlock must be kept open to both man and woman. Anyhow, the procedure to be adopted for the dissolution of marriage should be

different in their respective cases. This is the theory which represents the Islamic point of view, and the Muslim countries are partially following it.

So far it became clear that divorce has become a world problem as all grumble and complain about it. Those whose laws prohibit divorce totally complain of the non-existence of a way to escape from unsuccessful and unsuitable marriages. On the other hand, those who have opened the door of divorce, equally for both man and woman, complain about the growing rate of divorce and the instability of domestic life, and its harmful effects. Those who have given the right of divorce to men only express their dissatisfaction on two accounts: firstly, some mean people, after years of married life, unexpectedly divorce their old wives, simply because they suddenly feel eager to have a new wife. Secondly, some unchivalrous people refuse to divorce a wife, only to make her deprived of the possibility of a new marital life. Their conduct gives an impression to those who are not acquainted with the depth and the spirit of the teachings of Islam, that Islam has really allowed men to harass their wives as much as they like.

Here, we take up problem of ignoble divorces. Islam is strongly opposed to divorce. It wants that it should not take place as far as practicable. Those who frequently take a new wife and divorce the old one are denounced by Islam as the enemies of Allah. The Holy Prophet(S) has said: 'No permissible act is more displeasing to Allah than divorce.' The great religious leaders (Imāms) have abstained from divorcing, as far as possible. Here a few other questions arise. If divorce is so loathsome and so disliked by Allah, why has it not been totally prohibited by Islam? Islam could at least lay down certain conditions for its validity. The second question is: What does the sentence, 'Out of all permissible things, divorce is most detestable to Allah' mean? If it is permissible, it cannot be detestable and, if it is detestable, it cannot be permissible. Why does Islam look at a man who divorces his wife angrily and, why it does not prevent him?

In fact, marriage is a natural and not a contractual relationship. Nature has laid down special rules for it. Other social contracts like sale, hire, mortgage, peace, attorneyship etc. are mere social agreements. In a civil society the only natural law is the law of liberty and equality, on the basis of which all social rules should be framed. But in respect of a conjugal contract, besides the general principles of liberty and equality, nature has prescribed certain other laws also, which must be adhered to in the case of marriage, dower, maintenance and the last stage of the process, which is divorce. Marriage means attachment and union, and divorce means separation. Nature has designed the law of marriage in such a way that man acts with a view to appropriate woman, and woman withdraws with a view to fascinate and mislead man. Man wants to take possession of the body of woman and woman wants to captivate the heart of man. The foundation of marriage is laid on love, union and fellow-feeling, and not on mere co-operation and companionship. In the family structure, the fair sex occupies the central position, and her opposite sex the peripheral one. From all this it automatically follows that nature must have had special rules for the dissolution of family life also. A contract which is based on love and the feeling of oneness is not enforceable by compulsion. Two people cannot be forced to make sacrifices for the sake of each other! As we said, a wife occupies the position of a person deserving love and respect in the family order. If, for some reason, she loses that position and is deprived of the love and attention of her husband, the base of the family structure falls off and the natural order is deranged, and cannot be kept by law. Islam has urged woman to beautify herself to please her husband, to satiate his natural. It has also exhorted man to love his wife, to show kindness and attachment to her, and not to conceal from her his love for her. These steps have been taken to make the sexual enjoyment limited to the domestic atmosphere. All these steps have been taken with a view to keeping the family organization free from the danger of dissolution and disintegration. Here another question arises. If the wife's love cools down, will the domestic life be affected? Does it terminates the domestic life? If the lack of love on the part of the wife also terminates the domestic life, then naturally women should also have the right of divorce. In reply, it should be said that though the success of the domestic life depends on the mutual attachment of both the husband and the wife, there is a difference between the mentality of man and that of woman. Nature has placed the key of their mutual love within the control of man and woman's attachment to man is the result of man's attachment to her. It is man's apathy and faithlessness that cools down woman's love. On the other hand, woman's indifference and apathy does not affect man. Man's frigidity is the end of conjugal life, but woman's is not so. If man is sensible and faithful, he can always regain his wife's love by showing affection and kindness to her. It is not insulting to him to compel his annoyed sweetheart by force of law, to continue to live with him, and to pacify her gradually. But it is unbearable for a wife to resort to the force of law to retain her protector and the object of her love.

It is here where the westerners and their followers have gone in the wrong way. On the one hand, they create an atmosphere in which men pay little attention to their wives and sow their wild oats elsewhere and, on the other, they try to thrust their wives on them by the force of law. The present day Western world shows itself as enamored of 'equality', while as far as the family system is concerned, there exists something higher than equality. Instead of seeking the cure of the social ills and consolidating the family life, the Western world is weakening the domestic system and shaking its foundations and it is happy that it is advancing on the path of equality.

It is evident from the discussion so far made that Islam is opposed to divorce. Islam is strongly opposed to the ignoble action of those who divorce their old wives to have new ones. But, in the opinion of Islam, it is no remedy to force an unchivalrous man to keep his wife against his will. That is why we see that the cases of unchivalrous divorce are much less in number in the Islamic world than in the West. According to Islam, domestic peace is different from political peace. In this case non-encroachment on the rights of each other is not enough. What is required is the union of souls, which cannot be forced by law. Here two points should be noted.

First, from what we have written some people may wrongly conclude that we are in favor of allowing men to divorce their wives at their will and pleasure. Of course, that is not the idea. What we mean is that Islam does not want to use legal force against the husband. Otherwise, Islam welcomes every action which may dissuade him from divorce. Islam has intentionally prescribed such a procedure and has laid down such conditions for the validity of divorce that they automatically delay the dissolution of marriage and, in many cases, persuade the husband to give up the whole idea of separation. Islam has advised those who pronounce the divorce formula to do their best to dissuade the husband from the idea of divorce. Furthermore, a divorce is not valid unless it is pronounced in the presence of two qualified 'ādil (Just) witnesses, who are expected to make their utmost efforts to reconcile the couple. Anyhow, the necessity of the presence of two qualified witnesses is one of those factors which may dissuade the husband from divorce, provided this condition is observed strictly in its true sense. Islam does not regard this as an essential condition for the validity of marriage, which is the beginning of the marital contract, because it does not want to delay a good deed. Similarly, according to Islam, divorce is not effective during the woman's menstrual period, though there is no objection to the solemnization of marriage during that period. Apparently menstruation, being a hindrance in sexual intercourse, should affect marriage and not divorce. But as Islam encourages union and discourages separation, it has done so. And, even, it is necessary to wait for three months before a divorce is allowed. Furthermore, in the case of revocable divorce, the husband is permitted to resume conjugal relations during the period of probation *'iddah* (waiting period). Islam has placed another obstacle in the way of the husband, by imposing on him the expenses of marriage as well as those of the period of post-divorce probation for wife and of the care of children. This is, in fact, a great obstacle for man and depicts a horrible future for him. In addition to all this, Islam regards it necessary that in the case of the apprehension of breach and dissolution of family life, a family court consisting of two arbiters, one representing the husband and the other representing the wife, is constituted to arbitrate between them. It is preferable to select the arbiters from among the relatives of the couple because they are expected to know the causes of the dispute better and both the parties can talk to them freely and repose confidence in them. The accomplished jurists are of the opinion that arbitration is obligatory. And even Shahīd Thānī says that arbiters can specify certain conditions to dissuade the husband from breaking the marriage bond. A court of arbitration can direct the divorce offices not to finalize the action on a divorce case, till the court intimates them of its failure in bringing about peace and harmony between the husband and the wife. Anyway, any suitable action to dissuade the husband from repudiating the marriage bond is desirable in Islam, for because of this delay, causes of divorce may be removed and woman and man may resume their marital life.

The other point is that the unchivalrous divorce, besides dissolving the sacred family life, creates such other problems for the wife that they cannot be ignored. Here, in addition to man's faithfulness towards woman's sincerity, there are other questions such as becoming homeless for the wife, the question of handing over one's house to a rival and the question of the wastage of all her efforts and services in the past.

It should be noted that there are two causes for this problem and the main cause is the ignorance of Islamic rules and regulations. Most of the people suppose that all the fruits of woman's labor belong to her husband. They even think that the husband can force his wife to work for him and she has to obey all his orders like a slave. As we have repeatedly pointed out, woman has full freedom as regards her work and activity. Islam has given her economic independence. In addition, it has made the husband responsible to bear the expenses of his wife and children. Thus, Islam has provided woman enough opportunities, from the financial point of view, to lead a respectable life independent of man. Divorce and separation should not cause her any anxiety in this respect. Such misgivings are probably due to their own ignorance of the law.

Another cause of the trouble is the exploitation of the faithfulness of woman by man. Some women make sacrifices, not because they are unaware of the law of Islam, but because they are over confident of the sincerity of their husbands. They do not care to take advantage of the opportunity given to them by Islam. They are suddenly disillusioned and find that they have wasted their lives in making sacrifices for an unfaithful man and have lost the opportunity given to them by their religion. They should note that if a wife is expected to give up her legal right of keeping a separate account of her money and her earnings, the husband is also expected that, in consideration of her sacrifice and the service rendered by her, he should make presents to her and offer her gifts. As the Holy Qur'an says:

> When you are greeted with a greeting, greet with one better than it or at least as kind. (4:86)

It has always been customary among the good people to present the wife with valuable articles. Thus, the problem of becoming homeless is not related to divorce and that it cannot be rectified by changing the concerned law. This problem is related to the question of economic independence of woman and that question has already been solved by Islam.

Now, we will go to find whether Islam has provided a solution for the problem of undue refusals of some men or not. Divorce is the natural right of the husband, provided his relation with his wife run their normal course. Normally, if he wants to live with her, he should look after her, discharge all the rights belonging to her and treat her kindly. If he finds it impossible to live with her smoothly, he should pay up all her dues and part with her. Besides her dues, he is also required to pay her an additional sum as a token of goodwill and gratitude. The Holy Qur'an says:

> Provide for them, the rich according to his means, and the strained according to his means, a fair provision. (2 : 236)

But there may be cases when the conjugal life does not run its normal course. There may be a man who neither wants to live happily with his wife nor would he agree to divorce her. What should we do in this case? Many people are under the false impression that from the Islamic point of view, such a situation is incurable. They think that the woman has no alternative but to continue to suffer patiently till she dies! Islam is a religion which always upholds justice and such an allegation is against the principle of justice, which is a cardinal principle of Islamic law.

We think that divorce may be compared to a natural child-birth, which automatically takes its normal course. But when the divorce when it goes in an unnatural curse, is comparable to an abnormal delivery which requires a caesarean operation by a surgeon. This operation can be performed by a qualified judge only. Some deadlocks are not peculiar to the questions of marriage and divorce. They appear in other spheres also, such as those related to the financial problems. Suppose two people, through inheritance or some other way, come to own an indivisible article such as a vehicle or a painting and they are not willing to use it jointly or by turns. Neither of them is also ready to sell his share to the other partner. They also do not agree on any other formula for its use. In some cases, even they go further and decide to divide that article into two pieces which, evidently, makes it useless. In such cases, Islamic law allows the courts of law to intervene in such cases and put things right. The court can order the article in question to be let out or sold. The hire charges or the sale price will, of course, be divided between the owners.

Now let us go to the question of divorce. If a husband is uncompromising and does not discharge his duties and obligations, and at the same time, is not willing to divorce his wife, what action is to be taken? The judicial authority is allowed to intervene and should do so, to divorce the woman in spite of what man says. The Holy Qur'an says: 'Divorce may be pronounced twice: then either a woman must be retained in good fellowship or released in kindness.' (2:229) According to the Holy Qur'an, a husband has either to retain his wife and carry out all his duties and obligations magnanimously, or to release her and sever the conjugal bond. There is no third alternative, in which man neither divorces the woman nor retains her justly or magnanimously:

> Do not retain them [your wives] by force to harm them. (2:232)

Some jurists are of the view that these verses are applicable only to those husbands who want to revoke their divorce during the period of probation (*'iddah*). Though this verse has been revealed concerning maintenance and revocation, the context of verses as well as the relevant *ḥadīths* show that this is a general rule. The views quoted above, on the whole, prove that Islam does not allow any man to misuse his right of divorce and keep his wife as a prisoner.

Anyhow, it should be noted that every judge is not competent to intervene in such matters. Islam has laid down very hard and fast qualifications for a judge. It is worth noting that the cases of judicial divorce, made by the order of the Muslim judge, are exceptionally rare. Islam cannot allow the divorce to take the form that it has taken in Europe where the woman demands a divorce for the slightest excuses and the court pronounces a judgment in her favor.

As we said in the above mentioned chapter, Islam supports the fifth theory, according to which the way to divorce is open for both man and woman, but their way out is separate.

In conclusion, it should be said that though divorce as a natural right is peculiar to man, women who concern about their future may obtain the right of divorce as a proviso in the contract of marriage and make uses of it, if necessary. Thus, though Islam does not recognize that woman has any natural right of divorce, such right may exist as a contractual and delegated one.

Polygamy

Monogamy is the most natural form of matrimony. In this system the husband and wife each regard the feelings, sentiments and the sexual benefits of the other, as exclusively belonging to him or to her. The opposite of monogamy is polygamy which may assumes some forms.

Sexual Communism

Sexual communism means no exclusiveness. According to this theory, no man should exclusively belong to any particular woman, nor should any woman belong to any particular man. It amounts to complete negation of family life. History and the theories related to pre-historical times do not point to any period when man totally lacked family life and when sexual communism prevailed. In his book, *The Republic*, Plato has suggested a sort of family socialism for 'philosopher-rulers' and 'ruler-philosophers'. In the last period of his life, of course, he rejected this idea. Several leaders of communism in the 19th century also made a similar suggestion, but after some bitter experiences, several of the powerful communist countries officially recognized the law of monogamy in 1938.

Polyandry

Another form of polygamy is polyandry, viz. a woman having more than one husband at the same time. According to Will Durant this custom is found among certain tribes. Among the pre-Islamic Arabs also there existed some kinds of conjugal relations some of which may be regarded as instances of polyandry. For example, in one of them, to procure a better progeny for himself, the husband selected a man and asked his wife to allow him to have access to her for a fixed period. According to another custom, a group of men consisting of less than ten people, established a liaison with a particular woman. On becoming pregnant, she selected one man as the father of her child out of those who were willing to take that responsibility. The third kind of conjugal relations was known as prostitution. Anybody could have access to these women. If such a woman gave birth to a child, she called all those who had intimacy with her, and with the help of a physiognomist, determined who was the father of the child. Islam abolished all these three kinds. Montesquieu: 'On the coast of Malabar there lives a tribe called Nair. The male members of this tribe cannot have more than one wife, but the women are allowed to choose several husbands. Probably the reason is that, in this way, they may not be heavily burdened with family responsibilities and their professional efficiency may not be affected.'

Polygamy

It has been more commonly practiced than polyandry and sexual communism. It has not only existed among the pre-Islamic Arabs but also Jews the Jews, the Iranians of the Sasanian period and some Roman Emperors. In contrast to polyandry, Islam has not totally abolished polygamy, but has restricted it. In other words, it has fixed the maximum number of wives one can have. On the other hand, it has stipulated certain conditions and has not allowed everyone to indulge in having several wives. It is surprising that during the Middle Ages, when anti-Islamic propaganda was at its highest, the opponents of Islam used to say that it was the Prophet of Islam who, for the first time, invented the custom of polygamy. They claimed that this custom was the basis of Islam and the rapid spread of Islam among the various people of the world was due to it. At the same time, they claimed that polygamy was the cause of the decline of the people of the East. Based on historical evidence, Will Durant, of course, has shown that this is not a fact. For example, in Iran in the Sasani period, the number of wives which a man could have depended on his means. The number of women whom a man could marry was unlimited. During the pre-Islamic period, the Arabs could have an unlimited number of wives. Some Arabs, after converting to Islam, had to part with their wives except four of them.

Historical Causes of Polygamy

Now, we should find what the historical and social causes of polygamy are. But, firstly, we should see why polyandry and sexual communism were not successful. The main cause of the failure of polyandry and sexual communism is, firstly, that it does not suit man's his monopolistic spirit. Secondly, every human being is, by nature, keen to beget children and wants that his relationship with his past and future generations should be definite and satisfactory. Man's interest in his children is natural and instinctive. Polyandry, however, does not agree with this instinct of man. On the other hand, in the case of sexual communism, it is not possible to determine as to who was the father of that child.

Thirdly, polyandry is neither in her interest nor does it conform to her nature. There is no problem with polygamy for a man who wants a woman to meet his materials needs and satisfy his sexual instinct only. It is, however, inconsistent with the nature of a woman who wants to have spiritual relation with her husband. As we have already said woman needs man not only to satisfy her sexual instincts but also she wants a man whose heart she may control, who may be her protector and defender, who may make sacrifices for her and who may work hard and bring money for her. In the case of polyandry and sexual communism, however, woman cannot claim the love, devotion and sacrifice of any man. The money which a man pays to a prostitute or a woman earns through her own work and labor neither meets her requirements, nor has the same value as that which is given to her by the man who loves her.

Now, after analysis of the causes of failure of polyandry and sexual communism, we go to discuss causes mentioned for polygamy.

1- **Domination of Man**: Some people are of the opinion that this custom has come into existence as a result of the high-handedness and the domination of man and the subjugation of woman. As now the age of the high-handedness of man is over, the privilege of polygamy should, like many other false privileges, make room for equal and reciprocal rights of man and woman; and, if it is permissible for man, it should be permissible for woman as well.

We do not deny the factor of oppression as one of the factors which give a particular turn to history. We also do not deny that man has, throughout history, misused his domination over woman. But we believe that it is sheer short-sightedness to explain family relations on the basis of the oppression factor only.

If we admit this view, we must also admit that during the period when polyandry was popular among the pre-Islamic Arabs or among the Nairs, woman had got an opportunity to dominate over man and impose polyandry over him. But we know for definite that the pre-Islamic period of Arabia was one of the darkest periods in the life of woman. And, the custom of polyandry among the Nairs was not due to the domination or respect of woman, but was the result of the decision of society to keep the soldiers free from the burden of family responsibilities. In addition, among Western nations, during Middle Ages when patriarchy was at its climate and even up to fifty years ago when woman was financially supervised by man, why did not man's suppression lead to promotion of polygamy in the West? Thus, this cannot be the main cause.

2- **Economic Factors**: It is said that in ancient times, several wives and a large number of children were regarded as an economic asset. Man extracted work from his wife and children and treated them like slaves. Sometimes he even sold them out. Most of the slaves were not captured in battles, but were sold by their fathers.

It is evident that the sale of children is one of the cruelest and most barbaric human acts. To resort to polygamy for this purpose is as unlawful as this act itself. Even though, some primitive people had several wives with this idea that was not the case with all the people. In the ancient world polygamy was customary among the classes which lived with dignity and decorum. The kings, the princes, the chiefs, the divines and the merchants had several wives. As we know, these classes never exploited economically their wives and children.

3- **Geographical Factors**: Montesquieu and Gustave Le Bon insist that climatic conditions are the main cause of the development of polygamy. Montesquieu says: 'In tropical countries women attain puberty at the age of eight, nine or ten years and after being married, soon become pregnant. Because of a very early marriage, women in the tropics become old at the age of twenty. In the countries having a temperate climate women retain their charm and beauty for a long time. The husband and the wife become old almost at the same time. That is how equality between man and woman is established and men do not need to have more than one wife.' Gustave Le Bon is of the opinion that 'their physical and temperamental traits, their nursing of children and their ailments and diseases often force the women of the East to keep themselves aloof from their husbands. As the climatic conditions and the national characteristics of men in the East are such that they cannot bear even temporary separation, polygamy has become customary.'

It should be said that these explanations are in no way correct. The custom of polygamy is not confined to tropical regions in the East. During the pre-Islamic period this custom was common in Iran, where the climate is temperate. It is purely fictitious to say that in the tropics, women get old at the age of twenty, as alleged by Montesquieu. Secondly, if it is accepted that the early onset of old age in women and the intense virility in men are the causes of this custom, why did the people of the East not adopt the practice of free love and debauchery, as the people of the West did both during the Middle Ages and in the modern times. (In the West, as Gustave Le Bon has pointed out, monogamy is found only in the legal books and there is no trace of it in daily life, while in the East polygamy exists in its legal form.)

Will Durant gives an interesting account of the state of morality in Italy during the renaissance and says in Italy, it was a matter of pride not to have an illegitimate child, but to have one was not a matter of shame. In 1490, out of a total population of 90,000, there were 6,800 registered prostitutes in Rome. Of course, this figure does not include clandestine and unofficial prostitutes. Men, who enjoyed all the facilities provided by widespread prostitution, were attracted to marriage only if the woman concerned promised to bring a considerable dowry. Adultery was popular among married people and women thought that their husbands were allowed to have mistresses. Some people criticize the East for polygamy or *harems*, and regard it as a shame for the East. They should be told that what that existed in the East, with all its shameful aspects, is much superior to what that existed and still exists in the West.

By the way, it should be remembered that the absence of lawful polygamy among the Europeans, whether good or bad, has nothing to do with the religion of Christ, who never prohibited it. On the other hand, it confirms the rules of the Old Testament, which expressly recognize polygamy. Thus we can say that, in fact, the religion of Christ allows polygamy, and the ancient Christians have actually practiced it. Hence, the legal abstinence of the

Europeans from it must have some other reason or reasons, which will be discussed later.

4- Menses: Some others attribute polygamy to woman's menstrual periods and her aversion to sex during that time as well as to her exhaustion after child-birth and her desire to avoid sexual intercourse during the nursing period. Will Durant says that in the primitive societies women grow old quickly. That is why, in order to be able to nurse their children for a longer period, to lengthen the interval between their own pregnancies, they encourage their husbands to have a new wife.

There is no doubt that this places man and woman, sexually, in dissimilar positions and often makes men turn to another woman. But it alone cannot be a sufficient cause of polygamy, unless there exists some social or moral impediment preventing man from indulging in free love.

5- Limitation of the Period of Fecundity in Females: Some believe that the limitation of the period of fecundity of a woman and her menopause on the one hand and man's interest in having more children on the other, are among the causes which gave rise to polygamy. In such cases, if the husband does not like to divorce his first wife and at the same time wants to have more children, he has no alternative but to have a second, or sometimes even a third wife. Similarly, the sterility of the first wife may be another reason for the husband in contracting a second marriage.

6- Number of Members of Family: The number of

children a woman can bear is very limited, whether she has one husband or several husbands. But the number of children which a man can beget depends on the number of women he has at his disposal. It was a matter of pride for the ancient people to have a large tribe. It is obvious that polygamy was the only means of achieving that end. We think that all causes, which emanate from the dissimilarity between husband and wife as regards their sexual needs or procreation power may be only regarded as a legal permission; there are, however, more important causes according to which polygamy becomes an obligation of man and society and a right of woman.

7- **Numerical Superiority**: The last and the most important factor which has contributed to the emergence of the custom of polygamy, the numerical superiority of women over men. In this case, not only polygamy is permitted but also it is an obligation of men and a right of woman. To prove this point, two premises should be clarified: to prove the case two preliminary points have to be established. First it is to be proved that according to the reliable statistics the women eligible for marriage actually outnumber such men. The second point to be proved is that the actual existence of circumstances creates a right which married men and women owe to the women who have been deprived of marriage. The most important reason is that the number of the women eligible for marriage is always higher than the number of men so eligible is that the mortality rate among men has always been higher. There can be no doubt that at least in the primitive societies this was the position. In the today world as well, fortunately, almost authentic statistics exist. To prove this, we should also know the ratio between the number of men and the number of women eligible for marriage. In most cases this ratio is different from that which exists between the total population of males and the total population of females. For example, the statistics of 1950 shows that the number of women of marriageable age in America exceeded the number of men by about one million four hundred and thirty thousand. Bertrand Russell says that, in the present day England, more than two million women exceed men. It is said that because of the huge German casualties in the Second World War, the German Government had approached *al-Azhar* University to provide it with the formula of polygamy. Later it was learnt that following serious opposition by the Church the proposal had to be dropped. The Church preferred the privation of women and the spread of licentiousness to the system of polygamy, because this system is Eastern and Islamic! There is another reason for this difference according to which the onset of puberty in females is earlier. Practically in most of the countries of the world the husband is on an average five years older than the wife.

The mortality rate of men is higher, and deaths usually occur at the age when man should normally be the head of a family. It is seldom found that woman is among the victims. Whether it is a case of a clash between human beings or between man and nature, most of the victims are male adults. It is enough to realize that since the beginning of human history there has not been a single day when wars have not been waged and men have not perished. Further, the main reason why women have suffered less casualties is that men have always protected them and have themselves shouldered the most dangerous jobs, and there have been always imbalance between population of females and that of males, whether in the hunting age or in the age of agriculture or in the industrial age (if we accept that there had been such ages). Usually woman is healthier than man and has a greater power of resistance against disease. She is cured earlier. This has been proved in the light of scientific advances.

Now, let us find how the numerical majority of women of marriageable age not only creates a right for them but also an obligation for men and married women. There is no denying the fact that marriage is one of the most natural and most basic rights of human beings. Everybody, whether man or woman, has the right to lead a family life. For a woman this right is of utmost importance, for she needs a family life more than a man. As we have already said, to a man the material aspect of marriage is more important and to a woman its spiritual and sentimental aspect. If man has no family, he can at least partially fulfil his needs by indulging in free love and debauchery. But to a woman a family has a greater importance. Debauchery cannot even partially fulfil her material and sentimental needs.

After the establishment of the two premises, viz. the number of women eligible for marriage is larger than the number of men and it is a natural human right to have a family life, it is easy to draw the conclusion that if monogamy is regarded as the only legal form of marriage, a large number of women are bound to be deprived of their natural right. Bertrand Russell was conscious of the fact that in this case, a large number of women are to be deprived of their right of having children. He has suggested that women should be allowed to entice men and bear father-less children. As the father usually supports the children, the government should take his place and give a subsidy to the unmarried mothers. Russell maintains that woman needs marriage only for three reasons: to satisfy her sexual needs, to get children and to meet her economic requirements. The first two needs can be met on the sly. As for the third one, it should be looked after by the government. He forgets that woman wants that she should be under the protection of a loving husband and every child needs well-recognized parents and their sincere love and affection. Experience has shown that the mother seldom shows affection to that child of hers whose father is not known. How can the lack of this love be compensated? It appears that the British people have solved their problem without waiting for the enactment of Lord Russell's suggestion.

In the annual report, published by the Medical Department of the London Council, it was pointed out that out of every ten children born in the previous year one was illegitimate. The British Government instead of acting upon the advice of Lord Russell and solving the problem of unmarried woman has taken a step in the opposite direction. It has more than ever deprived woman of the male sex by legalizing homosexuality!

You will be surprised if you are told that the psychologists and the social philosophers in the West believe that man is born polygamous and monogamy is against his nature. Will Durant, explaining the present day moral chaos, says that much of it is due to our incurable interest in variety. Man by nature cannot be content with one woman. He says that by nature man is polygamous. Only the strongest moral restrictions and an appropriate amount of poverty and hard work, along with the external vigilance of the wife, can impose monogamy on him. A famous American researcher says that, unlike man, woman dislikes diversity and that is why she often does not submit to his overtures, but man regards diversity as an adventure. What is more important is that he is more interested in physical pleasure than in spiritual and sentimental pleasure. A French sociologist says 'one woman is born for one man, but one man is born for all women.' A biologist is of the view that a man's contentment with one wife weakens his progeny and hence this action amounts to an act of treachery against the human race; and, it is the system of polygamy made the children healthy and strong. We believe that the above description of the nature of man is not correct at all. These thinkers appear to have been inspired by the particular atmosphere prevailing in their own part of the world. Anyhow, we believe that both biologically and psychologically man and woman are dissimilar to each other and we confirm that polyandry is against her spirit. But we do not agree with the view that the spirit of man does not conform to monogamy. It is absolutely incorrect to say that his passion for diversity is incurable. To our belief the causes of man's unfaithfulness are related to the social atmosphere and man's nature is not responsible for it. In the Muslim East, on the one hand polygamy was permissible and, on the other, temptations and provocations to immorality did not exist. Therefore, true monogamy prevailed in most of the families. It is interesting that these thinkers say that man is polygamous by nature but should be legally monogamous. As a result, he has no more than one legal wife, but he can cohabit with any number of women he likes!

We believe that there is no doubt that monogamy is preferable, for monogamy means an exclusive family life. But when the number of women in need of marriage is greater than the number of eligible men, there are only two alternatives: either to officially recognize polygamy or to encourage unrestricted concubinage. In the case of the first alternative only a small percentage of married men will have more than one wife and all women in need of a husband will be able to secure a home and family life. In the case of the second alter-native will have sexual relations with several men, and thus almost all married men will become practically polygamous, and thus the institution of family will be destroyed.

In a society where women are not in a numerical majority, there is no need to polygamy. There are certain prerequisites to achieve this end. First of all, social justice should be ensured and adequate opportunities of suitable employment made available for every man, so that everyone eligible for marriage should be in a position to have a family life. The second condition is that every woman should be free to choose her husband and should be under no compulsion by her guardians or anyone else to marry any particular person of their choice. The third condition is that there should not exist too many temptations that seduce even women having husbands not to mention women having no husbands. But, if the women in need of marriage outnumber such men (bachelors), the prohibition of polygamy is a treachery to humanity. A woman who is deprived of her natural right a human being who is susceptible to psychic disorders and complexes and will think of taking revenge upon married women through seducing their husbands. It is here where the people who were more attached to the spirit of piety and chastity solved the problem by adopting the system of polygamy. Other people who were not so greatly attached to this spirit used the phenomenon as a means of indulging in debauchery. Of course, if someone thinks that polygamy, with all the legal and moral responsibilities it entails, is a bed of roses, he is sadly mistaken. From the angle of personal comfort and happiness, monogamy is definitely preferable.

Drawbacks and Defects of Polygamy

Now, that we discussed personal and social necessities making polygamy permitted, we would like to mention drawbacks and defects posed against it so that a general appraisal may be possible and, at the same time, it may be clarified that we admit that there are some problems with polygamy. But we do not confirm all objections posed against it.

From the Psychological Angle

The conjugal relations are not confined to such material and physical matters as bodily contact and financial support. The basis of conjugal relations is emotional and psychological (love, emotions and feelings). Love means the union of hearts and is not divisible. Hence, polygamy should not be permitted.

To our belief the above statement is exaggerated. It is true that emotions and feelings constitute the spirit of marriage. It is also true that feelings are not controllable. But it is pure fancy, rather a fallacy, to say that feelings are not divisible. It is not a question of dividing and distributing feelings in the same way as a material object is divided and distributed. It is a question of the mental capacity of man, which is not too limited to accommodate relations with two people. For example, parents having ten sons love all of them to the extent of worship and make sacrifices for them. Anyhow, one thing is definite. Love cannot be as intense in the case of several wives as it can be in the case of one.

From the Angle of Behavior

A woman usually regards the co-wife as her worst enemy. Plurality often induces wives to action against each other and occasionally against the husband also. It creates malice and turns the family atmosphere, expected to be an atmosphere of sincerity and serenity, into a veritable battlefield. Enmity existing between the mothers passes on to their children and the family atmosphere, instead of being the first school of moral training for the children, turns into a school of dissensions.

We believe that most of the evil effects are not the direct result of plurality, but are the consequences of its wrong implementation. Suppose a husband and a wife live together and lead a normal life. In the meantime the husband comes across another woman and takes a fancy to her. After a secret understanding between the two, the second woman raids the house and takes undue advantage of the husband, and challenges the authority of the first. But the things will be different and the internal conflict will be greatly reduced if the first wife knows that her husband is justified in having a second wife and that he is not fed up with her. The husband also must not assume arrogance, he should more than ever be kind to his first wife and should more than ever respect her feelings. The second wife also should remember that the first wife has certain rights which are to be respected. In short, all the parties concerned should remember that they have taken a step to solve a social problem. The law of polygamy is a progressive solution of a social problem and is based on the broader interests of the society. Those who execute it, should possess a standard of high-thinking and should be well-trained in the Islamic ways.

From the Moral Angle

It is said that polygamy means indulgence in sensuality. Morality demands that the gratification of sexual desire is minimized, for the nature of man is such that the more he indulges in sex, the more intense his yearning for it becomes, and even it may leads to homosexuality.

This objection can be looked at from two angles. Firstly, it has been claimed that sexual acts are repugnant to pure morality. It may be said that this view represents a wrong thinking. It has been inspired by Christian, and Buddhist ideas of morality based on renunciation. From the Islamic point of view, it is not correct to say that the less the gratification of sexual desire, the more moral it is. It is only excessive indulgence which is regarded by Islam as repugnant to morality. And, certainly, polygamy is not excessive indulgence. Thus, we also do not believe that polygamy is unnatural and a sort of perversion like homosexuality. As for the second point: that the more the natural desires are satisfied, the more they grow and the more they are suppressed, the more they are pacified, it is diametrically opposed to the current Freudian theory. From the Islamic point of view both the theories are false. Human nature becomes passionate both as a result of privation as well as unrestricted freedom. Anyway, neither polygamy is immoral nor is it against human nature to be content with one legal wife, and none of them causes human nature to become passionate.

From the Legal Angle

By virtue of a marriage contract both the husband and the wife belong to each other, and each of them has a right to enjoy the other. As far as the marital benefits are concerned, the marriage contract creates a sort of proprietary right. In the transaction between the husband and wife is, the goods under transaction, as marital benefits may be called, have already been sold to the wife. As such, if polygamy is to be allowed, its validity must depend upon the consent and agreement of the wife. She should have the right to decide whether she can or cannot allow her husband to have another wife. This means that to have a second wife is just as if a person had sold his property to a person and then resold it to a second customer. The validity of such a transaction will depend on the consent of the first buyer.

This objection is based on the presumption that the legal nature of marriage is that of exchange of benefits, and that each of the husband and the wife owns the marital benefits accruing from the other. Though this presumption is not sound, for the present we do not want to dispute it. This objection can be valid only in case the husband takes another wife only for fun. Obviously, plurality of marriage is not justifiable only so long as the wife can in every respect meet the lawful needs of her husband. But if there exists any of the justifying causes mentioned earlier, the objection becomes void. But if there exists any of the justifying causes mentioned earlier (menopause, sterility, disease), the objection becomes void. But if it is a social requirement, for example, if women outnumber men in a society or the society needs a larger population, plurality is a duty which is to be performed by an adequate number of men. It is a duty to be carried out to save the society from corruption and prostitution or to increase the population of the community. In such cases there is no question of the consent of the woman. Here, critics have looked at the question from a narrow angle (man's seeking for fun). We believe that in this case, polygamy is not acceptable, even if the first wife allows.

From the Philosophical Angle

The law of polygamy is repugnant to the principle of equality between man and woman as human beings. As man and woman both have equal rights, either both of them should be allowed to practice polygamy or neither of them. It is a pure and simple discrimination to allow man to have several wives and not to allow woman to have several husbands. This position is derogatory to woman and is not even in keeping with the Islamic view in respect of inheritance and evidence. In respect of giving evidence, two women are regarded as equal to one man.

Since we have already discussed the cases in which polygamy is justified, it is not necessary to dwell on this question any more. It seems that the critics have paid no attention to the individual and the social causes of polygamy. They think that it is only a question of passion. It is enough to say that the teachings of Islam in respect of polygamy, inheritance and evidence are different in different cases. In the case of inheritance it has allowed woman only a half of the share of man in some cases and an equal share in others. Similarly, in the case of evidence there has been different rules in different cases. All this shows that Islam has some other philosophy, which we have already explained.

Ḥarems

Another reason why Islam is criticized for polygamy is the system of *ḥarems* adopted by the former caliphs and sultans. Some Christian writers and missionaries have described polygamy in Islam as equivalent to the system of *ḥarems* with all its shameful and cruel aspects.

We have replied this question in the section concerning temporary marriage to some extent.

The point which should be noted here is that Islam neither invented polygamy, nor did it abolish it. Islam only reformed this ancient custom.

The first modification made by Islam in it was as follows. Before Islam, one could have an unlimited number of wives and could form a *ḥarem*. Islam prescribed a maximum limit. It did not allow anyone to have more than four wives. Those who had more than four wives at the time of embracing Islam were required to release the extra wives.

Another reform introduced by Islam was the condition of giving equal treatment to all the wives. Islam does not allow any discrimination between the wives or between their children. The Holy Qur'an expressly says:

> If you [ear that you will not do justice (to them) then have one only. (4:3)

The Pre-Islamic world observed equality neither between the wives nor between their children. We have already said that during the Sassanian period polygamy was customary in Iran. One or more wives were called favorite wives and they enjoyed full rights and others known as servant-wives had lesser legal rights.

Concerning justice in treating wives, there are many points narrated both in *ḥadīths* quoted from and *sīrah* of the Infallible. For example, in a *ḥadīth*, it has been said that husband and the second wife are not allowed to enter into a stipulation at the time of their marriage, by which the second wife agrees to live on unequal terms with the first wife. All that the second wife can do is to forego some of her rights for practical purposes. But no such condition can be stipulated, nor is it possible that she should not have equal rights. With all these strict moral conditions polygamy becomes a duty instead of being a means of pursuit of pleasure. To be fair, it must be admitted that the number of those, who observe in letter and spirit all the conditions (for example, justice) laid down by Islam in respect of polygamy, is very small. According to the Islamic law, if a man apprehends that fasting may be harmful to him he should not keep fast. You come across many people who inquire of you whether they should or should not keep fast. But the Holy Qur'an specifically says that if you fear that you will not treat your wives equally, you must have only one wife. Still you do not come across a single person who may say that he apprehends that he might not be able to treat two wives equally, and may inquire whether in his circumstances he should or should not have a second wife. It is evident that some people knowing well that they will not be able to do justice, still have several wives. These are the people who bring a bad name to Islam by their unworthy action.

Besides the condition of justice, there are also other conditions which a husband has to fulfil. A husband has the right of having more than one wife, provided his financial condition allows him to do so. Physical and sexual potentialities are another pre-requisite. It is reported that in case somebody collects several women, while he is not fit to satisfy them all, he will bear full responsibility if any of them takes to sin.

From what that has already said, it became clear that Islam has not disparaged women by allowing polygamy, but has protected their rights and prevented them from becoming worthless toys in the hands of men. Modern man is averse to polygamy, not because he wants to be content with one wife, but because he wants to satisfy his sense of variety and to escape from many duties and responsibilities, financial and otherwise. And Islam is against this.

Index

A

Adam, 38
al-Azhar, 111
'Allāmah Kāshif al-Ghiṭā, 61
'Allāmah Ṭabāṭabā ī, 26
al-Shifā, 27
ardor, 49
Aristotle, 45
Āyatullah Nā īnī, 26

B

Bernard Shaw, 14
Bertrand Russell, 111, 113

C

capitalism, 35
chastity, 49, 59, 61, 116
childbearing, 40
Christianity, 5
Civil Code, 9, 11

D

dignity, 9, 29, 33, 34, 41, 57, 106
divorce, XII, 10, 29, 49, 53, 58, 67, 74, 75, 86, 87, 88, 89, 90, 93, 95, 97, 98, 99, 100, 109
dower (*mahr*), 67, 69
Dr. 'Alī Shāygān, 5
dress, 25, 49

E

economic tool, 69
education, XIII, 33, 49
Einstein, 32
England, 2, 5, 111
equality, 2, 3, 4, 6, 7, 8, 29, 30, 33, 36, 67, 72, 84, 90, 92, 107, 121, 123
Europe, 2, 11, 80, 100
Eve, 38

F

family, X, XII, XIII, 1, 3, 9, 10, 11, 33, 37, 42, 43, 44, 49, 52, 54, 55,

INDEX

60, 64, 67, 78, 79, 80, 81, 83, 86, 87, 91, 92, 94, 95, 101, 102, 105, 106, 111, 112, 113, 115, 116, 118
family rights, 21, 42, 49
Fāṭimah Zahrā, 39, 64
fixed-time marriage, 51, 52, 54, 55, 56, 57, 58, 60, 62
Flexibility of Islamic Laws, 23

G

Germany, 5
Gustav Leabeon, 107

H

ḥadīth, 99, 123
ḥarems, 59, 61, 62, 108, 122
Human Position of Woman, 37
human rights, 2, 3, 8, 31, 41, 42
husband, 5, 10, 43, 48, 52, 53, 54, 55, 56, 58, 64, 65, 68, 69, 75, 76, 77, 78, 79, 80, 84, 86, 88, 91, 93, 95, 96, 97, 98, 101, 102, 104, 107, 109, 110, 111, 113, 116, 118, 120, 121, 123, 124

I

Ibn Sīnā (Avicenna), 26
'iddah, 53, 94, 99
identity, 18, 64
iftā, 49
ijtihād, XIII, 49
Imām 'Alī, 24
independence, XII, 4, 5, 18, 21, 63, 64, 69, 76, 81, 96, 97
inheritance, XII, 21, 29, 83, 84, 98, 122
Iranian Civil Code, 5
Islam, IX, X, XI, XII, XIII, 12, 13, 14, 15, 16, 17, 18, 20, 23, 24, 25, 26, 29, 30, 32, 37, 39, 40, 41, 49, 51, 61, 63, 64, 65, 67, 70, 72, 73, 75, 76, 77, 78, 79, 81, 85, 88, 89, 91, 93, 96, 97, 98, 99, 100, 102, 103, 119, 122, 123, 124, 125
Islam and the requirements of time, 16

J

Jean Jacques Rousseau, 2
Jesus, 39

L

laws, X, XI, XII, 5, 9, 11, 12, 14, 15, 16, 17, 20, 23, 24, 26, 37, 50, 51, 63, 76, 81, 85, 89, 90
liberty, 2, 3, 4, 6, 7, 33, 64, 65, 90

M

maintenance, 29, 49, 50, 67, 70, 72, 76, 77, 78, 80, 81, 85, 90, 99
Maintenance, 67, 78, 84
maintenance (nafaqah), 69
marriage, XII, 6, 10, 39, 49, 50, 51, 52, 53, 54, 55, 56, 57, 58, 59, 60, 61, 62, 63, 65, 67, 68, 71, 72, 73, 75, 84, 87, 88, 90, 93, 98, 100, 107, 108, 109, 110, 112, 113, 115, 116, 117, 120, 121, 123, 124
Modern Life, 13
modesty, 49
monogamy, 101, 102, 108, 113, 114, 115, 117
Montesquieu, 2, 102, 106, 107
morality, 34, 45, 49, 59, 108, 119
motherhood, 10, 49, 81

N

natural differences, 6, 44, 49
natural postulates of family rights, 42
Natural rights, 42
Nehru, 13
newspapers, 6
Noah, 38
nobility, 9

O

ownership, 5, 11, 37, 44, 75, 77, 78

P

penal rules, 49
Pharaoh, 38
Plato, 45
Polyandry, 104, 115
polygamy, 29, 58, 101, 102, 103, 104, 106, 107, 108, 109, 110, 111, 115, 116, 117, 119, 120, 121, 122, 123, 124, 125
Prophet, 17, 24, 39, 61, 64, 75, 103
Prophethood, 17, 39
Ptolemaic, 34

Q

Qur'an, 8, 17, 19, 24, 35, 37, 38, 39, 48, 61, 67, 71, 73, 74, 75, 97, 123, 124

R

The Republic, 101

responsibilities, 6, 7, 47, 54, 64, 102, 106, 117, 125
retribution, 7
rights, IX, X, XII, XIII, 1, 2, 3, 4, 6, 7, 8, 29, 30, 31, 32, 33, 35, 36, 37, 41, 42, 43, 44, 45, 47, 49, 64, 68, 72, 73, 76, 77, 78, 93, 97, 105, 112, 119, 122, 123, 124, 125
Russell, 113, 114

S

Satan, 38
Sexual communism, 101
sexual morality, 49
Shahīd Thānī, 95
Shī'ah, 5, 56
Shighār marriage (exchange of daughters), 63
social philosophy of Islam, 9
social standards, 9

V

Voltaire, 2

W

wife, 10, 38, 43, 48, 50, 52, 53, 54, 56, 58, 60, 62, 67, 68, 70, 73, 75, 77, 78, 79, 80, 81, 86, 88, 89, 91, 93, 94, 95, 96, 97, 99, 101, 102, 106, 107, 109, 110, 111, 114, 116, 118, 120, 121, 123, 124, 125
Will Durant, 4, 76, 102, 103, 108, 109, 114
William James, 5, 51
working, XIII, 24, 49, 79

www.ingramcontent.com/pod-product-compliance
Lightning Source LLC
Chambersburg PA
CBHW011317080526
44588CB00020B/2736